ETERNITY TO ETERNITY

ETERNITY TO ETERNITY

BEING

NOTES OF CONFERENCE

AT

BRISTOL

1931

LONDON

STOW HILL BIBLE AND TRACT DEPOT

22 PATERNOSTER ROW

MADE AND PRINTED IN GREAT BRITAIN BY PURNELL AND SONS
PAULTON SOMERSET) AND LONDON

CONTENTS

READINGS

ADDRESSES

NOTE

All quotations of Scripture where
they differ from the Authorised
Version are from The New Translation by J. N. D.

ETERNITY TO ETERNITY

I

READING

EPHESIANS I.

J. T. The Lord will help us, I think, in going over this heavenly ground, and perhaps it may be well to keep before us that, there being six chapters in the epistle, we may have one chapter for each meeting.

I have been thinking recently of the link there is between the epistle to the Ephesians and the ministry of David and Solomon. In this connection it is interesting to note that the prayer of Moses the Man of God has in view eternity; he says, "From eternity to eternity thou art God" (Ps. xc. 2), and David, in inaugurating the service of God in 1 Chronicles xvi., delivers a psalm which is formed of parts of several Psalms ending with the 106th, in which he says, "Blessed be Jehovah the God of Israel, from eternity and to eternity!" In bearing these thoughts in mind, we shall be able to see what is in view in this epistle.

1

The epistle brings before us what is really "from eternity to eternity", going back to the purpose of God and culminating in glory to God in the "assembly in Christ Jesus unto all generations of the age of ages". In David's psalm (1 Chron. xvi.), all the people *said*, Amen, that is to say, there is the suggestion of the saints being brought into agreement with what is stated, that is, of our being brought on to the ground of eternity—"from eternity to eternity".

P. L. So the Psalmist in Psalm cvi. 5 says, "That I may see the prosperity of thy chosen ones, that I may rejoice in the joy of thy nation, that I may glory with thine inheritance". Does that suggest the epistle to the Ephesians?

J. T. Exactly. Moses would link us on in Deuteronomy xxvi. with the purpose of God in the thought of "the basket"; and I believe a right understanding of Ephesians would enable us to understand what is typified by the basket; it is what the believer is from the standpoint of divine counsel. We shall recall that in Deuteronomy xxvi. the basket is said to be taken out of the hand of the worshipper and set down by the priest before the altar. That illustrates the abstract thought of the believer always being held in regard of divine purpose, and as in that dignity he is able to speak of his responsible origin, of what his father was, etc. Then it will be noted that the worshipper goes back to the first-fruits, and the priest is no longer mentioned; he sets the basket down before Jehovah and he worships. "From eternity to eternity" would signify that there is a dip down, and in that dip, God makes known what He is,—but the object is eternity.

H. H. "From eternity *to* eternity" covers all the period of *time*?

J. T. I thought so. The dip, so to speak, the down coming is to display what God is, and how He effects His purpose.

H. H. And that is what the scriptures deal with in the main, is it not?

J. T. Yes. In the period between the two eternities, there is the display of what God is, in the working out of His thoughts and the testimony here in the presence of evil, so that He might be known, but the great end is "*to* eternity".

C. A. C. It seems to bring us into the full scope of the divine thought.

J. T. The opening verses of the epistle clearly exhibit the idea of "from eternity": "Blessed be the God and Father of our Lord Jesus Christ, who has blessed us with every spiritual blessing in the heavenlies in Christ; according as he has chosen us in him before the world's foundation, that we should be holy and blameless before him in love; having marked us out beforehand for adoption through Jesus Christ to himself, according to the good pleasure of his will, to the praise of the glory of his grace, wherein he has taken us into favour in the Beloved". That is all, so to speak, "from eternity". Redemption is not brought in until after all that is stated; redemption involves the dip down.

H. D'A. C. Redemption was necessary because of what had come in in the interval. In eternal ages we were not viewed as sinners, but as persons chosen in Christ.

J. T. Yes. "The basket", to use the simple figure in Deuteronomy xxvi., refers to what we are according to the counsels of God. "A perishing Aramæan was my father" refers to the condition and time of responsibility, and all that terminates, for after speaking about his history and his fathers, the worshipper comes back to the basket.

Eu. R. Who is the priest suggested in the passage?

J. T. I think it is the Lord as securing the believer. That is what the Lord is set for. He is the minister of the sanctuary and secures us in conditions according to the light of purpose. That is presented in the abstract, in the priest taking the basket and setting it down before the altar; but afterwards reference to the priest is omitted, and the worshipper puts the basket down before Jehovah. That is to say, there is a full recognition of our responsible origin and history, and of redemption meeting all that condition. The passage here deals with that side of things: "In whom we have redemption through his blood, the forgiveness of offences, according to the riches of his grace" (verse 7).

M. W. B. Would you say the one is on the line of purpose and the other the line of the ways of God?

J. T. Quite so. Therefore, Moses and David in the types, are linked, the one ministry bringing us out of Egypt, involving redemption, and the other (including Solomon) setting us up as a habitation of God, growing to a holy temple, as seen in this epistle.

M. W. B. I wondered whether you would link the ways of God more particularly with chapter ii. verse 11 and onward.

J. T. Well, the earlier part of the chapter also deals with what we were, and speaks of the power of God; but we have to see that for the working out of the testimony here in

the church, we are first taken up to heaven:
"has raised us up together, and has made us
sit down together in the heavenlies in Christ
Jesus", ch. ii. 6. All that has in view the testimony down here, that the heavenly feature
should enter into it.

J. H. T. Would the baptism of John in
Acts xix. refer to the responsible side, and
then the men being baptised to the name
of the Lord Jesus and the Holy Spirit
coming upon them, link up with this? The
Spirit coming upon the twelve men would
enable them to enter into this.

J. T. Quite so. Those referred to in Acts
xix. were placed on the ground of Paul's
ministry, and the Holy Spirit being given
would enable them to enter into the heavenly
side, and it is similar with us. I think we
ought to distinguish between eternity and
heaven. "From eternity to eternity" is one
idea; but heaven has in view the testimony
here. It is a question of the predominance of
heaven. It is, of course, alluded to as the
abode of God, but that is all in view of His
relations with the earth.

Ques. You mean that heaven is not really
looked upon as a description of a past eternity?

J. T. No; it is part of creation. It is in
view of the testimony. I think all references

to heaven, and to elevation, are intended to impress us as on the earth. What God is, is infinitely beyond us. We may have some idea of moral elevation by seeing the heavens; they convey the thought, but there is the recognition in scripture that the heavens cannot contain God. (See 2 Chron. vi. 18.)

C. C. E. The heavens are all created.

J. T. God in grace seeks, through physical things, to convey His thoughts to our minds, but it is a great thing to reach a point where you are clear of mere physical environment. Spirituality involves that. I find it very difficult to get rid of physical environment in my thoughts, but I think spirituality involves that we do.

QUES. You mean we ought to get outside of any idea of a specific place for God?

J. T. He dwells in light unapproachable.

A. M. H. How do you regard the new heavens and the new earth?

J. T. The same idea is retained in them as in the present heavens and earth; they are created. They are seen in the eternal state of things (Rev. xxi.).

W. R. P. Do you make any difference between heaven and the heavenlies?

J. T. I should. The word "heavenlies" in Ephesians is a peculiar one. The end of chapter i. clearly shows it is above, where Christ is. I think it would be an intensification of the idea. Verse 3 says, "who has blessed us with every spiritual blessing in the heavenlies in Christ".

A. M. H. Is the idea something entirely above and different from the earth?

J. T. I think so, showing that our blessings are marked off, or distinguished, from blessings that others may have on the earth.

F. H. B. You were dwelling on the statement, "From eternity to eternity thou art God"; would that give you the idea of God being the beginning and cause, and then the end of all things?

J. T. That is what I was thinking, and this epistle develops that thought for us.

A. E. M. Would the apprehension of that be connected with maturity in the believer? Hence in this epistle you have the climax of the work of God.

J. T. I am sure that is contemplated in the work at Ephesus because it is the acme of Paul's work, so that the state of the saints clearly would warrant all this being opened up. I have no doubt the saints at Ephesus would say, "Amen." In Psalm cvi. it is, "Let all the people say, Amen!", but in i Chronicles xvi. they *said it*.

A. S. L.   What difference would you make between heaven and the heavenlies?

J. T.   The Lord is said to have entered into heaven itself. It is something distinctive.

QUES.   Is it defined in Colossians where it says, "The things which are above, where the Christ is sitting at the right hand of God"?

J. T.   Yes, I think so; only there elevation and power are more in view, as the terms "above" and "right hand of God" imply.

W. R. P.   Would you connect the thought of place with heaven, rather than the heavenlies?

J. T.   Yes. What is presented here is an intensified thought, not that we are *with* Christ, but that our status is "*in* Christ."

H. H.   Would you distinguish between the beginning of Genesis, "God created the heavens and the earth" and the scripture just referred to, that Christ is entered "into heaven itself"?

J. T.   I think all these expressions are used to convey divine thoughts and to fit in with our limited ability to apprehend things. "Heaven itself" would convey the thought in its totality. We have the "third heaven", but "heaven itself" would involve more than that.

H. H.   You would allow for what is spiritual in the expression "heaven itself", but the heavens, as created, do not suggest what is spiritual.

J. T. The sidereal heavens are material, but generally the realm of the spiritual is conveyed by the term "heavenlies", even as to what is satanic; we read of spiritual wickedness in the heavenlies. God is dealing with us with a view to our education, taking account of our limited powers of apprehension. After all, besides the heavenly bodies, what do we see? The idea is, something far above, which is intended to dominate, and in a convincing way, to convey the idea of our privilege and supreme blessing and exaltation. But to "go up", that is to enter upon these blessings, we must learn to be spiritual. The disciples saw the Lord go up.

W. J. H. The heavenly bodies are for "signs", pointing to something spiritual.

J. T. Exactly; that is one of the reasons for which they exist. In creation God formed a means of conveying His thoughts, as, for instance, when He "set" the heavenly bodies. We cannot say how long they had already existed; they were created as mentioned in Genesis i. 1, and in Genesis i. 17 we read God "set them". That indicates how God has set things so that He can call upon them for use as He needs them. So the heavens and the earth, and especially the heavens, really suggest the thought of dominance.

Matthew takes that up in a special way, emphasising the kingdom of the heavens.

The heavens and the earth are to be the scene of the display of divine purpose, and the idea goes right through; God never gives up that thought, and what will be in the new heavens and new earth, will be the result of what is worked out in the present scene.

Eu. R. Would Matthew be the working out of the principle of the heavens and the earth, in relation to the assembly?

J. T. That is the idea; the Lord says "My Father who is in the heavens".

M. W. B. Is the purpose of God linked with God Himself prior to creation, and then is creation a sphere in which that purpose can be wrought out?

J. T. Yes, and He was pleased to create that sphere as heavens and earth. In His wisdom He did that.

M. W. B. And He did so in order to convey certain moral ideas to our minds; but you link purpose with eternity and God, prior to all else?

J. T. That is my understanding of it. It is a question of God, of whom, and through whom, and for whom are all things. (Rom. xi. 36.)

The heavens, spoken of in Genesis i. were not affected by the catastrophe: "the earth

B

was without form and void". In connection
with the renewed earth, there was evidently
an additional heaven formed on the second
day which would be that which is nearest to
us, but all as a means whereby God would
convey His thoughts to us.

M. W. B. In what relation does the purpose of God stand to the world to come?
Would you distinguish between the two
thoughts?

J. T. What God purposed for us in love,
has its full answer in the eternal state of
things, but it comes into display in the world
to come, thus taking the form of testimony;
for the world to come is really to bring into
public display what God is effecting now.
We shall see that in this epistle, the main
body of which deals with the world to come.
Its teaching shews how God brings out here
on earth now, the excellence of this superior
thing, the assembly, and brings it out of
heaven. Chapter ii. contemplates that in the
ages to come God will set forth "the surpassing riches of his grace in kindness towards
us in Christ Jesus". What follows on that is
the habitation of God down here; that is to say,
the "habitation" depends on our having first
been raised up together and made to sit down
together in the heavenlies. "Raised up" refers

to elevation. This would promote unity; and we are to be here in unity for the habitation of God. All this, too, would tend to keep us small, for being great I can be small: "less than the least of all saints". Thus we are in God's hands as suitable for His present purpose.

A. S. L. That is the great effect; it enables you to be genuinely small.

J. T. In being small you are morally great, that is, you are like Christ:

> "O keep us, love divine, near Thee,
> That we our nothingness may know".

E. R. Do you connect the basket with the inheritance because it is heavenly?

J. T. It contains what is heavenly—the first-fruits,—and it is taken out of the hand of the worshipper by the priest. It represents what God has in mind as to us viewed in relation to purpose.

E. R. The person who brings the basket has the purpose of God in his thoughts, and values the inheritance.

D. L. H. He has the purpose of God in his basket!

J. T. That is better; because the man himself *is* the basket, figuratively speaking, but not as the Syrian; it is the man in the light of purpose. The basket is formally separated by the priest taking it out of his hands and setting it down before the altar. Then the man makes the confession as to his ancestry, and afterwards *he* sets the basket down and worships.

Ques. What about the basket in Exodus xxix.?

J. T. It is similar, having reference to the humanity of Christ as essential to priesthood.

P.L. In John xvii. you have the Priest in relation to the basket, the Lord lifting up His eyes to heaven, demanding that He might have His own with Him.

J. T. That is very good. The Father had given them to Him. The Lord thinks of them in relation to the testimony, and then that they might be with Him as He says, to "behold my glory which thou hast given me". In the first four verses He speaks of His mediatorial service, and then asks to be glorified with the glory He had along with the Father before the world was; that is surely "from eternity to eternity". In verse 6 He speaks of His disciples, and the greater part of the chapter deals with them in connection with the testimony here; and then He asks the Father that they should be with Him—to "behold my glory which thou hast given me, for thou lovedst me before the foundation of the world".

It is quite clear that verse 24: "I desire that where I am they also may be with me, that they may behold my glory which thou hast given me" is eternity in the future, and then He adds the past: "For thou lovedst me before the foundation of the world".

H. D'A. C. The glory of verse 5 is not communicated. But in verse 24 He says, "That they may behold my glory which thou hast given me".

J. T. "The glory which I had along with thee before the world was," verse 5, seems to be spoken of in our hearing, as calculated to produce holy adoration. It is evidently the glory of Deity—glory as between the divine Persons.

H. D'A. C. It is a very special privilege for us to hear of it in this way.

J. T. Verse 24 is the "glory which thou hast given me, for thou lovedst me before the foundation of the world". I thought the reference to "before the foundation of the world" was to link on eternity with eternity, that they agree. But verse 5, as remarked, seems to be between divine Persons: "the glory which I had along with thee before the world was".

A. E. M. The glory in verse 5 is not said to be seen.

J. T. We cannot say it is the same as verse 24, for the glory there is said to be *given;* the "glory which thou hast given me".

QUES. Would that be conferred glory?

J. T. If He says, "the glory which thou hast given me", I would leave that as it is stated. It refers to what has been given to Him as Man. He speaks of giving them a glory which the Father had given Him, which, of course, could not be essential Deity.

F. H. B. Is not the stress in verse 24 on the word "my"? "That they may behold my glory".

J. T. It is His as given, and His love for His own would have them with Him to behold it.

F. H. B. In verse 5 He receives it.

J. T. It may seem to amount to that, only the expression is: "and now glorify *me, thou* Father, along with thyself, with the glory which I had along with thee before the world was".

A. S. L. Is it not so, that having come into Manhood, even the glory that was His from all eternity He would receive now from the Father?

J. T. Verse 5 says "the glory which I had along with thee before the world was", apparently involving association. Elsewhere it is said that He comes in the Father's glory; but that would be revealed evidently, but the glory of verse 5 seems to be between the divine Persons.

J. J. Is that very much like John i. 1: "The Word was with God"?

J. T. Not precisely; though it would include that; John xvii. 5 is undoubtedly a reference to the Lord's status in Deity.

The mention of it should appeal to us, calling forth worship. "The glory which I had along with thee", He says. The preposition is very often translated "with", but "along with" intensifies it. As Man He returns to the status of Deity.

A. E. M. Is it like the Mediator passing for a moment out of our sight, and in that way establishing equality in status with God in glory?

J. T. I think it is. In verse 14 of chapter i. you have the same preposition, where it says, "As of an only-begotten with a father". There you have an object of affection in Manhood in relation to purpose; but John xvii. 5 seems to deal with equality of divine Persons.

E. R. Would you use the word "unity"?

J. T. Well, the idea is *alongside*, as of one your own equal. It is not what They are *towards* One Another, as in chapter i. verse 1. "The Word was with God" is another idea, the preposition is different; it is *toward;* but chapter xvii. 5 is "along with" as involving equality, I think. In John xvii. 1–4 mediatorial service is clearly in view, thus "glorify thy Son that thy Son may glorify thee", but verse 5 goes further and so there is emphasis on the personal pronouns "me" and "thou".

W. R. P. Why do you bring purpose into chapter i.?

J. T. In regard to the Only-begotten. We have here (Eph. i.) the Beloved; we are made accepted in the Beloved. That is where you get an Object for the Father's affections. We are now on the line of purpose, because we are on the ground on which others can be brought in. Sonship is really with a view to others being brought in. That is the idea, and John i. 14 has that in mind. The glory He had there, was the "glory as of an only-begotten with a father"; it is descriptive.

W. R. P. Then sonship is relative?

J. T. Clearly; it is to establish a ground for purpose, so that the position here is in the Beloved. Of course there is also the declaration of God in the Son.

M. W. B. What connection do you see between the Beloved as you are quoting the expression now from Ephesians, and John xvii. 24: "for thou lovedst me before the foundation of the world". Is there any connection between these two?

J. T. I think John xvii. 24 is to establish what we are considering to-day,—"from eternity to eternity". That reference is to bring in the love that was there. We shall see it in the eternity to come; the link is in love; that is, "eternity to eternity" is linked up by love; the One that was loved then is the Beloved in whom we are now.

J. J. Would you carry in your mind John i. 14, back into eternity?

J. T. No, I should not. It is a description of the Word as become flesh, as the passage most plainly states.

W. C. Do I understand that that was not an exclusive thought but rather descriptive?

J. T. Well, it is a human figure. It is not *the* Father, but *a* father: "as of an only-begotten with a father". He had that place, but to apply it to Him as in the Deity, would, it seems to me, disarrange the relations between divine Persons, because you must make room for the Spirit; but as soon as you come into the realm of divine operations and the accomplishment of divine purpose, you get sonship.

P. L. Is not that the very thing suggested
in John i. 1? "The Word was with *God*".
It would not do to say, the Word was with
the Father; that would leave out the Spirit.

J. T. I think we ought to see in the Son
becoming Man, One adequate for God to
express all that He is. No finite being would
be adequate for God to show how He can
love a person. I do not mean, of course, that
He did not love finite beings, but in the Son
you have a Person great enough for God's
heart. That is the idea you get in the baptism
of the Lord: "This is my beloved Son, in
whom I have found my delight". God has
an Object great enough to shew His love
family-wise, so as to lay the basis on which
we can all be brought into it.

E. J. McB. Is that why you stressed the
priest taking the basket in the first place?

J. T. I think the Lord takes the basket
just in that way. He knows what the Father
is set for, and He takes you, so to speak, for
that and never gives you up. He has taken
us up for that. It is abstract until you come
to verse 10 in the chapter (Deut. xxvi.). Then
I take the thing up myself and worship.

In the Son you have the Beloved. He has
"made us accepted in the Beloved". That
has eternity to come in view, but then we

come down to the working out of it all and that involves redemption.

Eu. R. What is the contrast between "in the Beloved" here, and what you spoke of in connection with status as being "in Christ?"

J. T. I think "in Christ" is more the dignity of the anointing. You need that in heaven. It is another thought.

Ques. Does the thought of Christ being loved "before the foundation of the world" involve family relationship?

J. T. I do not think so at all. We have to leave, in that respect, what was before the foundation of the world. There was relationship, of course, the relationship that exists between divine Persons. It is important to remember John i. has past and present tenses in dealing with this subject; what Christ *was* and what He *is*. What is stated in the present tense refers to Manhood, but what is stated in the past tense refers to Deity: "The Word was God."

A. S. L. What He was and what He became.

J. T. "The Word became flesh" (John i. 14). There you are on the ground of God working out His purpose.

H. H. Is there any direct reference to His Deity in Ephesians?

J. T. Of course it is assumed, but He is seen here as Man—the Object and Centre of the divine counsels.

H. H. Quite so; I was only thinking of what has often been said as to Colossians where there is very direct reference to Deity.

J. T. I think the scriptures in which the Deity of Christ is insisted upon are corrective. In heaven we shall never raise such a question; we shall be in the presence of God there.

C. A. C. "Who fills all in all" would involve His Deity, but it is said of Him as the exalted Man.

J. T. It is remarkable that the church is referred to in connection with that expression. The church is His fulness. How great is the thought that God should bring out such a thing in a Man! Who He is is evident.

A. S. L. We have certain scriptures methodically setting out the Lord's Deity, and having these we do not raise questions as to His Person; they are settled.

A. L. O. Would you not think the relations between divine Persons in eternity were greater than anything that has been revealed?

J. T. I should, certainly. If God is pleased to come within our range it is clearly unwise for us to say that what we see is all. I think it is due to God that we should leave Him, so to speak, in His own realm. If He has come into ours we adore Him, but we must recognize the mystery of piety.

A. S. L.   It is entirely beyond our competence to intrude into relationships that existed between divine Persons in eternity.

J. T.   God has been pleased to come into revelation. We must not forget that *He* has come; the ark of the covenant denotes the smallness of the compass into which God can come.

A. S. L.   Then there is one precious word from the lips of the Lord Himself we need to bear in mind; "No one knows the Son, but the Father" (Matt. xi. 27).

G. W. W.   You said something about corrective scriptures; what has to be corrected?

J. T.   In view of theology coming in, the Holy Spirit saw to it that the doctrine was there; there it stands; John i., Colossians i., and Hebrews i. remain, and all the theology of the world cannot overthrow what is there.

F. H. B.   We have to remember the creature can never comprehend the Being of God. He has revealed Himself for finite beings.

P. L.   So the Psalmist said: "who humbleth himself to look on the heavens and on the earth?" (Ps. cxiii. 6), and the previous verse is, "who hath placed his dwelling on high".

J. T. All that assumes revelation, but we must not limit God to that which that Psalm states.

Ques. Would it be right to say that love was there?

J. T. I believe love is the great thing in "eternity to eternity"; love was active before the world was.

J. J. And does not John i. 18 suggest the limitation of His revelation? "Who is in the bosom of the Father, he hath declared him". It shows that the revelation is limited to that, to the revelation of the Father.

J. T. I think the revelation involves *both*. "No one has seen God at any time; the only-begotten Son, who is in the bosom of the Father, he hath declared him". I believe the *Him* includes both God and Father. The Son is in that wonderful position, and so God is declared; the term employed is not "revealed" there but "declared"; it is declaration, and I think the position of the Declarer being mentioned is to bring out the advantage of it, that is, that He is in the *place of love*.

II

READING

J. T. In addition to what we touched upon
this morning in chapter i., it may be pointed
out that what is brought before us in the
chapter involves the will of God and the
power of God. Having come down to the
sphere of testimony, we have the subject of
redemption mentioned (verse 7) whence all
is worked out. The "administration of the
fulness of times" implies that all is to be
carried over as finished, or in a mature condition. Hence the apostle speaks of "all
wisdom and intelligence", and having spoken
of the "good pleasure of his will" he pro-
ceeds to allude to the "mystery of his will"
and the "counsel of his own will". The period
from Adam to Noah illustrates the working
out of these things; so that we have the expression, "the seventh from Adam", as indicating
full development, Enoch being translated; and
then, in Noah, the carrying over of the result
of the testimony, involving maturity; for all

25

that entered into the ark was mature; there was no idea of multiplication in the ark. All the living creatures came to Noah; and his sons and their wives were, of course, full grown. There were no children in the ark and nothing immature. In all this, too, there was the idea of mystery. The epistle to the Ephesians has maturity in view; what is going over is to be mature. The teaching of this epistle is to lead to that. Hence we read, "that we may be no longer babes" (chap. iv. 14). Maturity should ever be before us, especially as we draw near the end.

F. H. B. The apostle speaks in chapter iv. of growing up "unto a perfect man". Is that maturity of affection?

J. T. Yes. By the knowledge of the Son of God we arrive at the full-grown man. The Son of God being from God here in testimony, it is how He is seen here; we "grow up to him in all things". But I thought we might see in chapter i. the will of God—the "good pleasure of his will" and the "mystery of his will" and the "counsel of his own will". The "mystery of his will" involves obscurity on the part of those who have part in it.

F. H. B. Is the "mystery of his will" here connected with the world to come?

J. T. Yes; "to head up all things in the Christ, the things in the heavens and the things upon the earth". I apprehend these "things" to be fully developed, that is, each answers to the mind of God. One can understand that the lives of Enoch and Noah were mysteries. The testimony of Noah in the building of the ark and preaching would be mysterious to the then world. What was all this about? But it culminated in material being carried over in full maturity, so that another order of things is begun.

QUES. What have you in mind as to carrying over?

J. T. Well, that should be the attitude of our souls. Enoch "was not, for God took him". Taken in connection with Noah and the ark, Enoch represents the heavenly side. In the ark, we have the result of the testimony carried over out of one world into another. It was full of life, but mature life, as far as the facts shew.

P. L. Would the expression "the men whom thou gavest me" suggest maturity?

J. T. Exactly. If God has abounded, as it says, "towards us in all wisdom and intelligence, having made known to us the mystery of his will, according to his good pleasure which he purposed in himself for the adminis-

c

tration of the fulness of times; to head up all things in the Christ, the things in the heavens and the things upon the earth", it is clear that growth is in view; so that the next section of the chapter, the prayer of the apostle, is to the end that we might have the "spirit of wisdom and revelation in the full knowledge of him, being enlightened in the eyes of your heart, so that ye should know what is the hope of his calling, and what the riches of the glory of his inheritance in the saints, and what the surpassing greatness of his power towards us who believe". The mystery would be seen in those who are grown, who are in the light of the mind of God, who know how to hide it and are content in smallness here.

H. H. Would this suggest the perfection which is for God's world produced by the Spirit in the way of formation in the saints?

J. T. Quite so; the work at Ephesus evidently had this in view.

H. H. Paul stayed there for three years to be used of God in the development of all this amongst the saints there.

J. T. The divine thoughts presented in this chapter are brought to bear upon us so that there should be maturity, in mystery, so that there is contentment in obscurity, both in our

daily lives and in our service. In the knowledge of the place that we have in the divine
scheme, we can accept obscurity, so that an
Ephesian Christian is properly capable of
taking up Corinthians. The teaching here
involves smallness and obscurity outwardly.
The "seventh from Adam" would mean that
the testimony set out in Adam had developed.
It descended from Adam through Seth, not
through Cain: Abel's offering having come
in and Seth being appointed instead of Abel,
you have light descending from Adam. Adam
is set up again, so to speak, and Enoch is
the seventh, so that it is a development and
a development involving maturity, because
before his translation he had the testimony
that he pleased God, and he prophesied that
he saw the Lord coming with the holy myriads
(Jude 14). The heavenly testimony is involved
in Enoch and the earthly in Noah, but in
either case there is maturity, Noah suggesting
the idea seen in the four living creatures
(Rev. iv.), but Enoch is a disciplined or taught
man, corresponding with the twenty-four
elders.

QUES. Do you mean that the twenty-four
elders represent experience in divine things?

J. T. Yes; Enoch is the "seventh from
Adam", and his name signifies a disciplined

man, that is, a man who is taught of God; that is one side of the position. The other side is what God has secured in a living way which is seen in Noah and the ark, I think.

Eu. R. How do those two sides come into the scripture before us?

J. T. They enter into the idea of the mystery. There is the mystery of God's will; that would imply that certain things are to be carried through, but at the present time it is mysterious: the expression "for the administration of the fulness of times; to head up all things in the Christ", meaning that all the periods of testimony have rendered their quota. I thought that the period between Adam and Noah helped to indicate how God works all this out, the experience and intelligence in the heavenly being illustrated in Enoch, and what is living in Noah.

A. M. H. Are you suggesting that all these thoughts enter into the idea of the "mystery of his will"? (chap. i. 9).

J. T. Yes. As having a bearing on us here at the end. There should be intelligence through discipline and walking with God, and then the development of life. One idea in life is variety, and I believe that the idea of variety was intended to be conveyed in the ark. These thoughts have a bearing on our growth and spiritual instruction under the discipline of God, and the development of the affections that God intends to be displayed as expressive of life. All is according to "the counsel of his own will". There is, therefore, the will of God in its "good pleasure", its "mystery" and its "counsel".

J. J. Would all that lead on to Abraham, after Enoch and Noah?

J. T. Well, in Abraham you get a family taken up. In him God has a people, an inheritance.

J. J. Where would you place Abraham in the epistle to the Ephesians?

J. T. "The God of our Lord Jesus Christ, the Father of glory"; he comes in there. In connection with Abraham you have the God of glory. In result God has an inheritance, as we see in verse 18.

A. M. H. What is your thought as to counsel?

J. T. What comes out in the world to come, "the fulness of times", is in keeping with eternal purpose; "He *works* all things according to the counsel of his own will" (v. 11).

A. M. H. Then what is the difference between the "good pleasure of his will" and the "counsel of his own will"?

J. T. Both refer, I think, to the way things are worked out. The "good pleasure of his will" is evidently what He finds in us in this respect, as we had this morning. Then there is "the mystery of his will". I think the will is brought in to show that nothing can interfere with it; that all goes through. We get the family idea in chapter iii., that is, every family in the heavens and the earth is named of the Father. That would bring us down to Abraham in the types, but what I think we might see here, is the intelligence that is alluded to and what God has in the saints: "the riches of the glory of his inheritance in the saints" (v. 18).

Eu. R. In connection with what goes through, have you in mind that God would give us the sense in our service, of being linked up with what He had in His mind before the foundation of the world, and what He will display in the world to come?

J. T. Yes, that it is a question of His purpose and the counsel of His will, all is in keeping with eternal thoughts, only that it belongs to the sphere of testimony. It is on the way from one eternity, so to speak, to another; the fulness of times is the result of all the testimonies.

C. A. C. Do you connect this with what was spoken of this morning as the dip down?

J. T. That is what I was thinking. Redemption was reached: "In whom we have redemption through his blood, the forgiveness of offences", and then the entire will of God is worked out.

QUES. Is that connected with Revelation x. 7 "the mystery of God should be finished"?

J. T. Pretty much so, only Ephesians touches our intelligence in regard to what God has in His mind, and what He works out in the sphere of testimony before entering the eternal state. The "administration of the fulness of times" is the culmination of testimony on the part of God, what He can do: "to head up all things in the Christ, the things in the heavens and the things upon the earth".

A. M. H. What is your point as to that?

J. T. Well, I think "things" are used to convey the thoughts of God: "The invisible things of him are perceived, being apprehended by the mind through the things that are made" (Rom. i. 20). They refer to the concrete thoughts of God, in whomsoever they may be seen.

C. A. C. Have you in mind maturity of a spiritual character?

J. T. That is what I was thinking. That is what God is working for; there is the development of intelligence in His school as in Enoch, so that we please Him, and there is the development of sympathy with Him that it arouses in our hearts while in a world of corruption. Enoch had the testimony that He pleased God before his translation, but he prophesied, saying, "Behold, the Lord has come amidst his holy myriads" (Jude 14). And then the working out of life, not in a childish way, but in a mature way, regarding each other in affection. Hence, in the type, the ark was full of intelligent varieties of life. I think it would have been one of the most interesting studies for any one who understood life to have gone through the ark and have seen, not life maturing, but the life matured.

C. A. C. So that there is all the substance for glory to God in the assembly.

QUES. Would that maturity be developed in every one in eternity?

J. T. It is to be developed *now* or never. Do not put anything forward or you will be very small.

D. L. H. "That we may be no longer babes".

J. T. Yes; "until we all arrive at the unity of the faith and of the knowledge of the Son of God, at the full-grown man, at the measure of the stature of the fulness of the Christ."

J. H. T. In the ark there were seven of every clean beast, and two of every unclean; why do the unclean come in?

J. T. It is not unclean in the sense of what is evil, but rather that they would be of *some* use. They would not be carried over if they were bad, but the sense is conveyed of the great preponderance of what was to be for God in the way of sacrifice.

W. R. P. You said just now that you get the thought of maturity of life in the ark and also of variety of life; would you say something about that?

J. T. I was saying that maturity of intelligence was seen in Enoch. He walked with God for three hundred years. What an experience that was! What an opportunity for acquiring a knowledge of God, and God was pleased with his companionship for He took him to Himself. But then the idea of variety is not there. Variety is in Noah, the full result from the creation in the way of life; and that, I apprehend, would now be the working out of affection.

W. R. P. Is variety seen in developed affections?

J. T. "In your faith have also virtue, in virtue knowledge, in knowledge temperance, in temperance endurance, in endurance godliness,

in godliness brotherly love, in brotherly love
love"; the latter is mature love (2 Pet. i. 5–7).

C. A. C. Is it not referred to in this epistle
as the "life of God"? (iv. 18).

J. T. That is a very remarkable expression; perhaps you would tell us something
about it.

C. A. C. I suppose the "life of God"
would be love in activity.

J. T. Therefore the unregenerate are
alienated from it "by reason of the ignorance
which is in them". That "life of God" is
here amongst the brethren; it is moral; the
life of God in this sense has come within the
range of men; but unregenerate men are
alienated from it. Would you think that?

C. A. C. Well, yes; and in that life the
inheritance can be possessed and enjoyed.

F. H. B. Do you understand that God is
working now to form that which is to be
carried over, the present work of God?

J. T. Quite so, that is the maturity that
this epistle aims at.

F. S. M. How is that maturity developed?
What would be conducive to its development?

J. T. I think what was quoted from Peter
helps, having one thing in another; having
in your faith virtue, and in virtue knowledge, temperance, endurance, godliness and

brotherly love, and then love. I think love there, is the height of maturity; that is to say, you correspond with God. It is in having these things, one in the other, that we develop maturity; hence, brotherly love is balanced by love; love is of God.

S. J. B. C. You would not be restful with brotherly love. There is a danger of loving one another more than God. You reach God in love.

J. T. Love is the "bond of perfectness" and it is reached thus in a mature way, according to Peter's instruction.

W. L. Does it suggest that all those things presented in Peter are there in germ, but not developed?

J. T. I think it is by having the one in the other, you develop perfectness. It is not exactly that you could have faith without love, but the point is you have all the things in relation to each other.

F. H. B. That would give the idea of a complete man.

J. T. I think it would. We shall see later how we are to be imitators of God, to "walk in love, even as the Christ loved us"; there is correspondence with God. I think there is a great deal of immaturity. Whilst there is a good bit of light amongst us, growth is what the Lord would impress upon us, so that if He carries us through it will be as mature.

QUES. Had Mary in John xii., arrived at it through discipline, especially that of chapter xi.?

J. T. I should say so; she is marked not only by love but by intelligence as to what she does.

QUES. Would you say the living creatures in the ark convey the thought of maturity?

J. T. They were capable of multiplication when the time came, but not in the ark; there is no evidence of any multiplication or dominion, it is just what was there in a mature way. So spiritually we may visit the ark and we see the varieties of life going through. I believe that is what would be attractive as a testimony to others; it is the variety of life.

F. S. M. It is significant as to Enoch and Noah that it was said of each of them that he walked with God. Is that an essential quality for both heavenly character and spiritual maturity?

J. T. Quite so; and the animals came to Noah. It is remarkable the sympathetic link there was; with the dove particularly; she returned to him and he took her unto him in the ark.

W. W. Do they suggest the matured thoughts coming into the minds and hearts of the saints?

J. T. Quite so. I think the "things in the heavens and the things upon the earth" refer to certain thoughts of God concretely presented. We have the idea of a family later but the things in the heavens and on the earth headed up in Christ, would mean a mature, intelligent state of things. "In him", it says. Those thoughts are being, so to speak, brought out concretely; now in mystery, but presently to be seen in full maturity headed up in Christ.

A. M. H. Why is the thought of "heading up" in Christ?

J. T. It refers to maturity, what we are speaking of. If I am to be headed up I have respect for the idea of headship. In David's ministry you get that emphasised. It is remarkable the number of times you get the word "head" in 1 Chronicles; and in the last chapter of the book it is applied to God. David says, "thou art exalted as Head above all" (1 Chron. xxix. 11).

Therefore, the "mystery of his will . . . for the administration of the fulness of times; to head up all things in the Christ" would mean a developed state of things, in which

the thoughts of God are presented concretely.
It is no longer their being apprehended in
the material creation, the "invisible things of
him" will be seen in their full significance
headed up in Christ. Everything that men
are occupied with, that may have had origin
with God, will be seen then in its true meaning.

A. M. H.   It is maturity corresponding with
headship.

J. T.   That is the thought.

J. H. T.   Is that why you have seven adults
in the ark corresponding to Noah in headship?

J. T.   You mean the three sons and their
wives and Noah's wife; quite so.   There you
get maturity and we can be assured that every
creature in the ark was in keeping with that.
There is not the slightest evidence of any
rebellious conditions.   I believe the idea of
headship permeated everything.

E. C. R.   So, would the idea of attraction
be seen in the creatures coming two by two
unto Noah into the ark?

J. T.   They came to the person, and so the
dove came back to him and he took her to
him into the ark.

P. L.   It says, "They went to Noah, into
the ark, two and two of all flesh, in which
was the breath of life"—(Gen. vii. 15).

Would that be suggestive of the movements of life?

S. J. B. C. I suppose that power of attraction is open to the weakest believer.

J. T. Is not that a leading feature of John's ministry, the principle of coming to Christ? "No one can come to me except the Father who has sent me draw him" (John vi. 44). We come under spiritual influence. John's ministry makes Christ an Object of attraction, on the principle of life.

M. W. B. In which way is variety of life developed?

J. T. Well, we have to go back to the roots. God created variety, and, spiritually, every root for God must be in Christ. Take David. Christ is the "root of David".

C. A. C. Then the variety is distributed over the whole company of saints; "to every one of us". There is variety coming out in the gift of Christ to each one of us.

Eu. R. Why in chapter ii. does he take the Jew and the Gentile back to their past state at the beginning?

J. T. I think it is to bring out what he had already started with in the second part of chapter i.—the power of God. There is the "knowledge of him", which is a thing we should notice; that we should have "the

spirit of wisdom and revelation in the full
knowledge of him"; (verse 17) and then,
"what is the hope of his calling, and what
the riches of the glory of his inheritance in
the saints, and what the surpassing greatness
of his power towards us who believe, according to the working of the might of his strength,
in which he wrought in the Christ in raising
him from among the dead".

C. A. C. Does that bring in the thought
of the "Syrian ready to perish"? Does
chapter ii. rather take up that side of things?

J. T. I think so, both in verse 1 and verse
11. So the first half of chapter ii. is to show
the evidence of the power of God in those
who, as it says, were "dead in your offences
and sins, in which ye once walked according
to the age of this world, according to the
ruler of the authority of the air, the spirit
who now works in the sons of disobedience:
among whom *we* also all once had our conver-
sation in the lusts of our flesh, doing what
the flesh and the thoughts willed to do, and
were children, by nature, of wrath, even as
the rest: but God, being rich in mercy, because
of his great love wherewith he loved us, (we
too being dead in offences), has quickened
us with the Christ". That is a question of
the grip of evil in which we were held, and

the power of God taking us out of that; and then going to the full height of blessing, as it says, "and has raised us up together, and has made us sit down together in the heavenlies in Christ Jesus". So that, in the first part of chapter i., we have the will of God, and then in the second part the power of God applied to Christ and in chapter ii. to us, so that we are seated in the heavenlies. It is not here exactly a question of our eternal portion, but in view of testimony, as verses 7–10 show.

Eu. R. In what way does seated in the heavenlies have in view the present testimony?

J. T. It is to lend lustre to us as down here. It is "in Christ Jesus", notice, not "with Christ". It is with one another in that exalted position, in the status of "in Christ Jesus"; heaven is very conversant with the idea of the anointing, and our position there *in Christ* alludes, I believe, to the great dignity we have in the anointing. It is not a question yet of the family, but of the place we have in the anointing, which heaven would understand. The angelic companies understand that; and it is to give heavenly lustre and dignity to us down here. That, I think, is what chapter ii. means.

Ques. Is that connected with divine sovereignty?

D

J. T. It is, surely. It speaks here of the great love wherewith God loved us and His rich mercy. He has in view the setting out of a testimony in us here, now, and in the future.

F. H. B. You spoke of an Ephesian Christian being able to take up the Corinthian position in testimony; is that the thought?

J. T. That is what we may see. It is persons—not yet a family, as I understand it, but rather the dignity connected with the anointing in heaven, our being in Christ and there unitedly; so that there is not a created being in heaven, that would not respect us. It is the status we have, as I may say, officially.

W. J. H. Stephen with the face of an angel would be understood by the angels. The dignity of the anointing was seen in his face.

J. T. Was not the heavenly dignity there in the most palpable way before the council, the superiority of the man? It was "as the face of an angel".

M. W. B. Some of us have linked testimony with the present, and display with the future. How do you link testimony with the future?

J. T. It will be seen in the assembly. You have here "display in the coming ages", I

apprehend that in the coming world we shall
be dignified in an official way. "In Christ"
is our status, and this chapter gives us that:
"In the heavenlies in Christ Jesus". There
is also what goes with it, the glory of God,
which would mean the divine nature worked
out in us. In the assembly coming out of
heaven there certainly is testimony. I believe
the members of the church will be employed
universally, but in this dignified way, as in
the anointing.

C. A. C. Is not that really essential to the
body and the habitation of God at the end
of the chapter?

J. T. I think it is. I do not see how you
can have the habitation of God down here,
without this dignity. It marked the tabernacle,
and it marked the temple. The tabernacle
was dignified by the anointing and the temple
by the wood, gold, etc.

P. L. Was this thought set out in Wisdom
in Proverbs viii.? "I was set up (or anointed)
from eternity".

J. T. Yes. If God comes in to operate
there must be that. It is the idea of repre-
sentation, and I think the greatest thought of
it for us, is in this chapter where He has
"raised us up together". That brings in a
peculiar link between us, "has raised us up

together, and has made us sit down together in the heavenlies in Christ Jesus". Think of the myriads thus seen! They are sitting. It is their place and there is not a dignitary in heaven who will not regard them accordingly.

A. M. H. That bears on our position down here. If we are to form the habitation of God, this necessarily enters into it, as also into our service in the millennium.

G. W. W. Why does it say in chapter i. that we are blessed "with every spiritual blessing in the heavenlies in Christ", and here that we are made to "sit down together in the heavenlies in Christ *Jesus*"?

J. T. I suppose "Christ Jesus" has a bearing down *here* in view of testimony. "In Christ" carries with it the idea of status or dignity that we have in *heaven;* and in which we are blessed.

I think the Ephesian feature enters into Corinthians. If I sit down to partake of the Lord's supper as in Corinthians, abstractly I am an Ephesian; I never lose sight of that. I do not need to bring that forward *at once.* As we may see in Deuteronomy xxvi. the basket is set down by the priest. Well, there it is, but immediately I am talking about the Syrian. I am, however, going to speak about the basket.

J. O. S. "Created in Christ Jesus"; would that be the basket?

J. T. I think so. Notice, it is "in Christ Jesus". The new man is "created in truthful righteousness and holiness". That is not a question of status but of *quality*.

D. L. H. When the man puts down his basket, does he not say I am in the good of that now?

J. T. I think he does, and he has got the first-fruits there too. I understand it is that I hold myself in that light, and the Lord as Priest takes that on; but it is, so to speak, in abeyance until the time comes in the meeting to bring it forward, but it is there all the time.

Eu. R. Does it involve the work of God?

J. T. It does, but it is the believer taken up in the light of counsel. Therefore, you are a sort of dual being, not exactly dual personality, but you are viewed as in Christ abstractly, and, therefore, there is nothing attached to you at all as to responsibility. It is important, if I am to be in the assembly in the light of eternity, that I know how to analyse as to what belongs to that, and what belongs to the position of responsibility here. So I leave that, and I come to this, and then I go back to that. That is the order of the assembly. The basket is taken out of his hand

and set down by the altar; and then he speaks about his father and about Egypt, and then he goes back to the basket, and he worships. That is to say, he worships in relation to the basket and what is in it, and that is what God seeks. He wants us, not in a mixed condition down here, but in the light of purpose.

J. H. T. At the close of that chapter in Deuteronomy it says, "that thou shouldest be a holy people to Jehovah thy God, as he hath said". Is that the public result?

J. T. Quite so. At the end of chapter ii. we see how all this position in heaven enters into what is for God here. In verse 18, it is said, "for through him we have both access by one Spirit to the Father": that is how we stand down here; and then further, "ye are no longer strangers and foreigners, but ye are fellow-citizens of the saints, and of the household of God". You can see how the status we get in heaven enters into this.

W. W. As to verse 16—"and might reconcile both in one body to God by the cross"— I was thinking that involves the saints being set together for the good pleasure of God.

J. T. You will observe it is "by the cross"; Ephesians gives you reconciliation in connection with the greatest reproach in this world. It cuts at the roots of all special links amongst the saints and it is "in one body". This means that we are linked up in a positive way, but under the greatest possible reproach.

H. H. Would you say a word as to the end of this chapter ii.—the habitation of God in the Spirit is a present reality, is it not?

J. T. That is how it stands. "So then ye are no longer strangers and foreigners, but ye are fellow-citizens of the saints, and of the household of God, being built upon the foundation of the apostles and prophets, Jesus Christ himself being the corner-stone, in whom all the building fitted together increases to a holy temple in the Lord; in whom ye also are built together for a habitation of God in the Spirit". We have the general thought up to the last verse, but in verse 22 I think he has in mind the position of the church among the Gentiles: "In whom ye also are built together". It is the general position of Jew and Gentile first, but I think the Gentiles are the habitation of God by themselves, which would continue. We can hardly speak to-day of a habitation of God formed of Jew and Gentile, but we can speak of "ye also", that is to say, Gentile believers.

C. A. C. That is very interesting.

H. H. God has still His habitation on earth in spite of the failure there is at the present time.

J. T. And even although there may be few Jews which is perhaps so now. It was not so then; they probably formed the major part then, but now they are hardly able to be found.

H. H. This epistle was addressed to a Gentile assembly.

J. T. Quite so.

QUES. What were you going to say on verse 18?

J. T. Only to point out that we have come to that. "For through him we have both access by one Spirit to the Father". It is the principle of access in a positive way by the Spirit. It includes Hebrews x., but goes beyond it. Verses 17 and 18 shew that Christ has brought God to all in the gospel and that through Him we have access to the Father.

EU. R. Why do you get in verse 13, "But now in Christ Jesus ye who once were afar off are become nigh by the blood of the Christ"?

J. T. In Christ Jesus there is our status here on earth, the blood having removed all that would keep us at a distance. "In Christ Jesus" gives the Gentiles a place of equality with the Jews.

III

READING

J. T. What I believe the Lord would stress in this chapter, is the relation of the apostle to the things of which he wrote; and the depth of spiritual wealth that was there in him as reflecting what is in Christ,—"the unsearchable riches of the Christ". It will require perhaps a little more spirituality to lay hold of this feature; but in relation to the ministry it is quite clear that God intends, whilst presenting these thoughts to us, that there should be an understanding of what spiritual wealth there may be; for unless the ministry is accompanied by spiritual wealth, there is not much to commend it. This epistle contemplates the gospel as that of "the unsearchable riches of the Christ". The gospel was never intended to be presented in spiritual poverty. So that, whilst the ministry of Peter was in abeyance in the early record in the Acts (chap. v. to ix.) there was the clear evidence of the body of spiritual

51

wealth that he represented; whilst younger
men came forward, such as Stephen, Philip
and others, there was extant this spiritual
wealth. Of Peter it is said that his "shadow"
was a feature. That would point to his
spirituality. I think we may see a similar
feature here in the apostle alluding to himself as "I Paul". The name meant much
to the Ephesians, and he being a prisoner,
enhanced it.

M. W. B. Do you link the idea of spiritual
wealth with the condition of soul in the one
who ministers?

J. T. Yes.

M. W. B. So the spiritual conditions were
seen in Acts v. to ix. as a kind of basis for
the ministry.

J. T. I think so, especially as younger men
came forward more capable of active service.
God would maintain spiritual wealth, even
although it may not be in the persons meant
to be specially active in the ministry. In
connection with Peter's shadow it was in the
minds of the persons who brought out their
sick into the streets on beds and couches, that
they might come under it, which I think is
very remarkable; one's shadow may be more
valuable than one's preaching at times. Then
in Paul's case napkins taken from his body

effected cures, showing what precious substance was there. How valuable the body was as under the influence of the Spirit—the body kept under, so that the Spirit pervaded it and not the motions of the flesh.

A. M. H. Are you connecting the spiritual wealth with the saints as a whole and with the minister in particular?

J. T. With the saints as a whole; but the person who ministers certainly ought to be marked by it.

A. M. H. Just so. Would the state of the saints as a whole be indicated in the expression "faithful in Christ Jesus?"

J. T. Exactly, but the apostle wished to lead them forward; he prayed for them in two connections. They needed, not acquired knowledge so much as the "spirit of wisdom and revelation in the full knowledge of him"; and then they needed strengthening "in the inner man".

M. W. B. What would answer to the shadow of Peter now? Would it be our spirit and influence,—our bearing?

J. T. I should think so. We have a reference in Canticles that helps: "I sat down under his shadow with great delight" (ii. 3). That would mean that the speaker sat under the influence of Christ, and it would involve a shield from other things, so that she was restful.

W. J. H. I suppose you could not have a shadow without substance somewhere.

J. T. That is true. In Acts v. it contemplates spiritual substance, otherwise you could not have had a shadow with healing virtue. Then in Paul's case the napkins were taken from his body. That, I think, would bring in touches of love; hands using those napkins for cures—would regard with affection the precious body of the apostle.

Rem. And that took place at Ephesus, where "God wrought no ordinary miracles".

E. R. The saints at Ephesus would be greatly affected by his saying that he was prisoner on their account.

F. H. B. What do you understand by spiritual substance? Would it be spiritual formation in the person?

J. T. Yes. Peter and Paul were representative of the ministry in its fullest measure. It marked them both, characterizing their bodies. Romans contemplates that the body is to be devoted to God, a "living sacrifice", and the Spirit in it would be life; so that evidently the Spirit is to influence the body of the Christian.

H. H. All this comes into line with the greatness of Christ, the One who is set forth in this epistle. Spiritual wealth is resident in Him.

J. T. Yes. As I was remarking, the ministers reflect what is in Christ, the "unsearchable riches of the Christ". Ephesians contemplates what is unsearchable. It speaks of "the love of the Christ which surpasses knowledge". It is well to accept that we cannot compass these things, but we can know that they are there, and enter into them to such an extent that they are seen in us.

W. W. "Of his fulness we all have received" (John i. 16). Does that stand connected with what is on the line of the unsearchableness of the glad tidings of the Christ?

J. T. Quite so: "Of his fulness we all have received, and grace upon grace". It is a question of what we have received. What we are considering to-day is what marks the minister and whether the wealth is there, as a testimony. We can compass it in Paul; he is desirous that the Ephesians might know the extent of his knowledge of the mystery.

W. J. H. The apostle did not desire that the saints should think of him above what they saw him to be.

J. T. It is remarkable how he brings in "Paul" in the epistles. In one, "Paul the aged", but here it is "I Paul". Then he is the "prisoner of the Christ Jesus", meaning that the Lord had taken him aside in this way for certain ministry, that doubtless he could not have rendered otherwise; he is in a peculiar position. That is another thing that we ought to note, that one is not in one's position by choice. He is the "prisoner of the Christ Jesus": there might have been some other thought in his mind, but the "prisoner of the Christ Jesus" brought him effectively under the Lord's hand, where he would render the service that was needed. The epistles from Rome are all suggestive of this; that is to say we get the very best from brethren who are in positions entirely aside from their own wills or predilection. It is the "prisoner of the Christ Jesus". In the next chapter it is the "prisoner in the Lord" but here he is referring to the Lord's purpose in imprisoning him.

M. W. B. Would the "prisoner of the Christ Jesus" have the ministry in view, in contrast to the "prisoner in the Lord"?

J. T. I think so. It was also that the Lord might work out in him to the full the idea of the anointing, and that in it there would be that kind of man. "Christ Jesus" is the anointed Man, and this feature would work out in the prison.

P. L. Would "his bondman John" (Rev. i. 1) represent the same idea, the best obtainable?

J. T. Exactly; he was "in the island called Patmos, for the word of God and for the testimony of Jesus". He went there evidently under compulsion; he was a prisoner in Patmos.

J. H. T. Would Philippians help? "But I would have you know, brethren, that the circumstances in which I am have turned out rather to the furtherance of the glad tidings, so that my bonds have become manifest as being in Christ in all the prætorium and to all others" (i. 12, 13).

J. T. That amplifies this. Notice there he is the prisoner "in Christ", but here he is the "prisoner *of* the Christ Jesus". Initially, the Lord imprisoned him, but ultimately he was "in Christ" in the prison. Thus he was dignified in it. They might have thought he was a felon, but he was not that; he was "in Christ". Then in the next chapter he was the "prisoner in the *Lord*", not *of* the Lord. It is remarkable that knowledge should have come into the palace. It shows how if the Lord imprisons us, He will work it that it becomes apparent that we are not there as felons, but in relation to His will.

J. J. Even the wicked spirits in Ephesus could say, "Jesus I know, and Paul I am acquainted with" (Acts xix. 15). It was just after the napkins and aprons were brought from his body that that incident occurred.

J. T. Those seven sons of Sceva were terrible instruments for evil. But it is most touching to think of the apostle's body: "I bear in my body the brands of the Lord Jesus" (Gal. vi. 17). That is a touching thing, and anyone taking off those napkins would see those brands.

A. S. L. How delightful is the way he refers the brands to the Lord Jesus, not to those who inflicted them.

QUES. Would they convey an impression of the love of Christ in His death?

J. T. Yes. In Galatians the apostle made a point of what was there before their eyes in that respect. Jesus Christ was "portrayed", it says, "crucified among you" (iii. 1).

A. S. L. The thought in Galatians vi. 17 is of the slave branded by his master.

J. T. The Galatian false teachers would emphasise the circumcision and the marks that it would make in the body, that is, current religion accepted by men.

A. S. L. That is an interesting contrast; circumcision makes its mark, but Paul had the brands of *his* Master.

J. T. All the epistles given to us from Rome point to the wealth that marked the apostle in those circumstances. The wealth of the saints is not in their writings but what is in themselves. This works out through their bodies as a testimony.

QUES. Is there a reference to all this where it says, "They took therefore the body of Jesus"?

J. T. He "was with the rich in his death". Joseph and Nicodemus cared for the Lord's body in the most touching manner. What they brought bespoke their thought of the body of Jesus. Angels also were attendant, "one at the head and one at the feet, where the body of Jesus had lain", shewing the respect that heaven had for it; and relatively it is the same with the minister of Christ. I suppose Joseph of Arimathæa and Nicodemus, persons not marked off in the testimony hitherto, represent the work of God for an *emergency;* the emergency is a test, and the work of God answers to it. That precious body was exposed to wicked handling, but they become the undertakers of it, and Joseph went in to Pilate and demanded it, using, I judge, the advantage of his position. He had access through that.

QUES. It says that he was a secret disciple; has that any suggestion that he had in secret

E

been appreciating the value of Christ in His body?

J. T. No doubt; the credit is in the word "disciple", not in the secrecy of it, but he was a disciple and John's gospel takes great pains to bring out the work of God. However small the measure, it comes out in an emergency.

J. J. Would the incident of the woman who touched the hem of His garment show the substance that was in the Lord?

J. T. I think that is an analogous passage; the virtue came out of Him, and there, I think, you have the idea of church formation. The virtue that goes out of Him is really the germ of the epistle to the Ephesians, that the body is *of* Christ.

REM. "Do ye not know that your body is the temple of the Holy Spirit which is in you?"

J. T. That is the basis of the wealth we are speaking of.

J. J. Would you say why this whole subject of the mystery is put in parenthetical form in this epistle?

J. T. Evidently the apostle did not have it in his mind in the outline he had before him, but his heart became so full that he would have the saints know of his personal wealth in relation to that of which he is speaking.

F. H. B. What does he refer to in speaking of the "promise in Christ Jesus"? (verse 6.)

J. T. I suppose it refers to what God had promised as included in His purpose. Promise is on a lower ground than purpose, and I think it contemplates need or desire, either known to God or to those whose it is.

A. S. L. Would it refer at all to that gospel promise made to Abraham: "In thy seed shall all the nations of the earth be blessed"?

J. T. I think so; and there was "the promise of life" even before that.

M. W. B. With regard to your remarks, do you think the place Paul takes in this chapter emphasises the greatness of mediatorial service, the fact of it being seen in a vessel?

J. T. I think the mediatorial feature enters into the ministry, because this epistle contemplates that the preaching is by Christ: "coming, he has preached the glad tidings of peace to you who were afar off, and the glad tidings of peace to those who were nigh", but it was largely through Paul. I believe what is in view is, that the minister is so marked by spiritual wealth, that the unsearchable riches of Christ are brought concretely within the range of his hearers.

E. J. McB. So that he says, "my tribula
tions . . . which is your glory". We se
thus what the apostle suffered, and thi
enhanced the wealth of what was in his min
to bring to the brethren.

J. J. Would the same principle be true i
Corinthians? He suffered greatly for them.

J. T. Yes. There was strong feeling agains
him. It was extraordinary that his ministr
evidently was accepted but he himself refused
so that by the Spirit he brings himself befor
them, more than in any other epistle.

Ques. Why was the apostle anxious tha
the saints should understand his intelligenc
in the mystery of the Christ?

J. T. It is advantageous to us all if any
one (whoever or wherever he may be) ha
special spiritual intelligence. It belongs to all
What we should see is that Christianity in
volves a community, and whatever is ther
belongs to us all; that, I think, is what is i
view. The Ephesians were to know what
wealth of intelligence there was in the ministe
through whom the light had come to them

A. L. O. Would the one who is of Chris
Jesus, as you suggested, be the one likely t
get the spiritual manifestation?

J. T. I think he would. The apostle mus
have had wonderful times in the prison.

was, therefore, interested in the address last night, because it brought in an elevated line. The manifestation of divine Persons is what gives colour to Christianity. Who can tell what experiences the apostle had in those prison days? In writing this letter,—for instance, what light flooded his soul! How near the Lord was to him!

Ques. It is encouraging that neither Paul himself nor the saints are losers on account of his prison conditions.

J. T. His experience must have been most painful, at times, but what seasons of spiritual enlargement he must have had!

Rem. We have to accept the prison conditions if such are to work out for the furtherance of the testimony.

J. T. I think so. In John xiv. the Lord says, "My Father will love him, and we will come to him and make our abode with him". But *where* is he? His position would be according to divine ruling. That is what you see in the apostle here. His position as a prisoner was in Christ. The Lord knew where he was, and would go to him in those circumstances; and the apostle needed it. When Onesiphorus came to him, how pleased he was! We might think, if Paul were in London to-day, we would all flock there to see him, but they did not do that in his days; they did not seek him out very much. This is remarkable, but he valued the man who did. He "sought me out very diligently, and found me". What we should see in the epistles is this wealth of spirituality in the minister. How flooded with light he was, and how in keeping with it!

J. J. How completely it sets aside the mere professional side of service. It is the real thing here.

J. T. Well, the Lord has a word for us in that. There is much light, but spirituality is wanted—the body of spirituality to correspond with it.

Ques. Could you define what spiritual wealth is and how it is obtained?

J. T. I believe it is in getting to the Lord that a question like that is really answered in the soul. He will not leave us in the dark. When He went into the house in Matthew xiii. His *disciples* came to Him; He did not ask them to come. They wanted an exposition of what He had been saying, and He gave them the exposition of the particular parable they mentioned. Then He began to speak to them about wealth; first of all about treasure hidden in the field, and how He sold all that He had to buy the field. The acquirement of wealth involves sacrifice. How much it cost Christ that we might have wealth. It is the principle of giving up to get what abides. Then He goes on to speak about the merchant, a person who knew what refined things were, such as a pearl. A pearl is a thing that belongs to refined taste, and the merchant would know its value and would look for goodly ones. He found one pearl of great price, and again He sells all to get it. That is the idea that the Lord would impress upon us, that wealth is acquired at certain cost. Then He asks them, "Have ye understood all these things?" and they said, "Yea, Lord"; and He says, "every scribe discipled to the kingdom of the heavens is like a man that is a householder who brings out of his treasure things new and old". That is the line. He has got the new things and the old things, and he is not selfish about them. He treasures them, but he brings them out and shows them. Now, that is the real test in ministry. What can one bring out and show of new and old things, out of his own treasure? He is a householder, meaning that he cares for things and has them in their right places. That is, I believe, what the Lord would speak to us about.

Rem. That involves the work of God and not merely light.

J. T. It does.

J. J. Would the wealth be found in the prayer in this chapter?

J. T. Yes; the prayer refers to "the riches of his (the Father's) glory" (verse 16). Earlier the apostle says, "To me, less than the least of all saints, has this grace been given, to announce among the nations the glad tidings of the unsearchable riches of the Christ, and to enlighten all with the knowledge of what is the administration of the mystery hidden throughout the ages in God, who has created all things, in order that now to the principalities and authorities in the heavenlies might be made known through the assembly the all-various wisdom of God, according to the purpose of the ages, which he purposed in Christ Jesus our Lord, in whom we have boldness and access in confidence by the faith of him". You can see the lines on which wealth is acquired; the particular thing he is dealing with, was hid in God.

QUES. Would this at all bear on what the apostle says, "I know a man in Christ . . . such a one caught up to the third heaven"? Would you not see the deep reservoir of wealth there?

J. T. That would add to Paul's wealth, but I do not think he refers to it here. It is a question of what is revealed and that means

that I may have the "new" things; as also
the "old" things, which would mean that I
go back to the dispensations in which light
began to shine—from Adam to Noah; from
Noah to Abraham, and from Abraham to
Moses, and from Moses to David; the things
brought out in these eras should be acquired.

M. W. B. Is that why the expression is "the
administration of the mystery", referring to
what is worked out?

J. T. That is the thought. Administration
is from God's side. It was committed to Paul.
The result is that the principalities and powers
in the heavenlies see, in the assembly, what
the divine thought is at the present time; they
see the "all-various wisdom of God". There
are the "treasures of wisdom and of knowledge" (Col. ii.) in the mystery, but here it
is the "all-various wisdom of God" in the
assembly—the highest conception of wisdom
for heavenly intelligences to see worked out;
and this in such as ourselves! It goes beyond
even Proverbs viii. and ix. What a thought
it is for us! And so the apostle's prayer in
this chapter has reference to the *inner* man;
we need power inwardly to apprehend the
marvellous things presented.

H. H. Why do you say it goes beyond
Proverbs viii. and ix.?

J. T. Because it is "all-various". You do not get this in the creation of the material worlds.

A. S. L. Is it the idea of Joseph's coat of many colours? But what about that in connection with the actual state of the church down here? Does that affect the view that the principalities have?

J. T. Of course it does. What exists to-day must becloud the "all-various wisdom of God". This is a humbling consideration.

QUES. What is the distinction between the thought of the body and the assembly in this chapter?

J. T. Whilst formed of persons called out, the assembly contemplates intelligence. "I speak as to intelligent persons" (1 Cor. x. 15), that is, we are formed in the knowledge of God. This is furthered by the "spirit of wisdom and revelation". Therefore, what is done in our "care meetings" and "assembly meetings", as we speak of them, is intended for the angels to see; it is the working of love, but love acting wisely. Love is, so to speak, the background of wisdom; wisdom is its handmaid. So the existence of love amongst us will lead to things being done wisely. Love expresses itself in the wisdom of its ways.

M. W. B. Do you think there is a reference here to the expression in chapter i. 8, "which he has caused to abound towards us in all wisdom and intelligence"?

J. T. I should say so. What a thing the assembly is!

M. W. B. All is in view of there being a vessel here in which there is an answer to God, abounding to us in those remarkable attributes.

J. T. Exactly; so you can see that love must be the great feature in the assembly, and wisdom is the way it acts. 1 Corinthians xiii. helps to this as showing how love acts. It is not wisdom there. What is done is wisdom, but it is love's actions. Wise actions are love's actions; it is the same with God. What He does is in wisdom because of His love.

A. J. G. Does this thought of the "all-various wisdom of God" emphasise the necessity for the variety of life?

J. T. I think it does. Life is a necessary feature, but I think love is the greatest expression of life.

REM. In Galatians it says, "By love serve one another" (chap. v. 13).

J. J. Would you bring Psalm cxxxix. into this "all-various wisdom of God"? "In thy book all my members were written; during many days were they fashioned, when as yet there was none of them".

J. T. Quite so; they were "curiously wrought in the lower parts of the earth". That is formation, but this is more than that. It is not divine workmanship exactly in this chapter; what the apostle is alluding to here, is what we do; that God has brought about such intelligence in men here in the assembly, that His "all-various wisdom" is wrought out in them.

W. J. H. You were going to contrast the wisdom of God in creation with the "all-various wisdom of God" here.

J. T. In creation the material was inanimate, there was no love. It is a question of the material that God was handling, and of course there was wonderful skill in the creation, but the material did not lend itself to what God is Himself. "The invisible things of him are perceived, being apprehended by the mind through the things that are made, both his eternal power and divinity" (Rom. i. 20), but that is not His love. The material did not lend itself to that; but when one divine Person became a Man, then you have love acting wisely. Every thing that the Lord did and said was in wisdom; what He said, and what He did not say, was in wisdom.

The assembly is of Christ: "Of him are ye in Christ Jesus, who has been made to us wisdom . . ."; that is objective. We learn it in Him, so that the gospels are the great lesson book for us as we begin to think of acting in wisdom; it is how *He* acted. The Holy Spirit sent down from heaven is from Jesus up there, so that the body is formed; but the idea of the *assembly* involves persons— not simply an organism—and persons formed in divine intelligence, so that they *know what to do*.

A. S. L. It is only in Ephesians that the church is viewed as in the heavenlies: "To the intent that now unto the principalities and powers in heavenly places might be known by the church the manifold wisdom of God".

J. T. We are raised up together and made to sit down together "in the heavenlies in Christ Jesus". The angels bow to that; and they would look for the results; because the idea is the anointing, the status we have there; so that, as down here, the angels recognize the dignity of the persons forming the assembly.

A. S. L. The church in the heavenlies, is the church really at the full height of God's thought for it, and that cannot be interfered with.

J. T. I think, as presented in Ephesians, it is to bring out the dignity of the anointing as it is up there. We are raised up and seated in the heavenlies *in Christ Jesus*. It is dignity we have up there; it is dignity in the supreme place, which angels would understand, and they could follow the working out of the thing on earth in *such* persons.

C. C. E. What is the connection with "God, who has created all things"? What is the particular reason of that being brought in here?

J. T. I think in connection with what we are dealing with, the question of wisdom; because the wisdom seen in all God's operations is cumulative. The physical creation is wonderful, a thing to be apprehended by *faith*, not by the telescope. "By faith we apprehend that the worlds were framed by the word of God" (Heb. xi. 3). That means that His mind was already coming out, and involved wisdom; Proverbs deals with that. Wisdom was His nursling, showing that wisdom was already operating. We should not overlook the wonderful skill seen in creation; in fact Corinthians says that nature teaches us.

J. J. Would it not show too that all created things have a moral import behind them?

J. T. "The invisible things of him are perceived, being apprehended by the mind through the things that are made"; that supposes intelligence, hence, it is "by faith we apprehend that the worlds were framed by the word of God". That is a question for our minds, not for our affections. I do not think the creation is an object for my affections, but for my mind. It is a wonderful lesson book for the mind.

H. H. Do you think you have Christ prospectively in Proverbs viii. where it says, "Jehovah possessed me"?

J. T. We ought not to be too pronounced in speaking of that as Christ. It is a reference to Christ, but you cannot say it is He in an absolute way; wisdom is a quality.

A. S. L. It speaks of wisdom being "brought forth" there.

J. T. I think it is to emphasise what we are speaking of: the "all-various wisdom of God"—how important it is. Of course, its expression is in Christ, but it is not well to go beyond that, that it was necessary in the creation. Of course, we know from the New Testament that the creation was by Christ, not only as an instrument, but in His own power (John i. 3). In Colossians i. 16 the preposition involves His own power, but Proverbs is dealing with wisdom as a leading feature that comes out in the creation. It

was a quality operating in material things,
but now it has taken form in incarnation, in
Christ. But as here He was not dealing with
material things but moral things—with persons, not with particles. Wisdom created a
thing out of nothing really. What wisdom
was required to do that, and to poise the
universe and set it as it is before our eyes!
But Romans says that the mind apprehends
behind that, the "invisible things of him",
so that Proverbs has to be read in that connection. Of course in Proverbs wisdom also
deals with moral things. Solomon being
peculiarly possessed with it, and so a type
of Christ, in the main applies wisdom to
human circumstances.

A. S. L. "Thou shalt see my back parts,"
He said to Moses.

C. C. E. When it says in Proverbs, "When
he prepared the heavens I was there", the
He was really Christ.

J. T. It was He who actually did it.

C. C. E. Does that give the understanding?

J. T. I think it does. The Person that
prepared the heavens was Christ, and wisdom
was there.

G. W. W. Therefore, in reading Proverbs
you have to bear in mind that the Jehovah
mentioned there was the Jesus of the New

Testament. The passage cannot be understood unless that is borne in mind. That puts wisdom in its right and proper place before the soul.

J. T. I think it does. It is Christ in a sense, who is said to be the wisdom of God and power of God; it is really a quality or attribute. When it says, "wisdom hath built her house", you get beyond the physical creation. It points on to the church.

W. C. Would you say a word as to how wisdom came out in the Lord Himself? It speaks of Him being "filled with wisdom" and then He "advanced in wisdom and stature".

J. T. I suppose it was the divine thought that wisdom should show itself in the way He acted in every stage of His life here; so that as born He is cast upon God, and then at the age of twelve years He is in the temple in the midst of the doctors hearing and asking them questions. That was a very wise way to act, and an example for young persons—hearing and asking; and they were astonished at His understanding and answers. Then He goes down and is subject to His parents, and we do not hear of Him again until He is thirty years of age; and, according to Luke, He is apparently the last to be baptised of

F

John, and when He was baptised, He was praying. That is the attitude; and then He is anointed, the Holy Spirit comes upon Him. So that, following up His ministry (it would be impossible to go over the details) wisdom was seen in every word, every breath, every movement showing who He was, but everything was done rightly. You could not conceive of one thing but as rightly done.

W. C. Would that bring us to the "all-various wisdom of God" in the assembly?

J. T. There is nothing in the assembly that does not come out of Christ.

QUES. If the assembly is thus the vessel of that wisdom and a lesson book for angels, should it not add dignity to our walk here?

J. T. It should, and that is the reason why the apostle prays: "For this reason I bow my knees to the Father of our Lord Jesus Christ, of whom every family in the heavens and on earth is named, in order that he may give you according to the riches of his glory, to be strengthened with power by his Spirit in the inner man". I think we come here to the great burden that rested on the apostle in regard to the saints, our being strengthened in "the inner man". It is a spiritual thing:

'that ye may be fully able to apprehend", not exactly in intelligence as in chapter i. but in *inward power*. This prayer is that the power of the Father's Spirit should work in us, so that we should be fully able to take in divine things—viewed here in their full greatness. It is a question of ability inwardly.

H. H. The power which wrought *for* us in the end of chapter i. now works *in* us; the power "which he wrought in the Christ" and which also set us in the heavenlies, is now working *in* us.

J. T. That is working in us to bring about ability to take in divine things. There is "breadth and length and depth and height"; so that we are to be able to stand, as it were, in the very midst of the divine sphere of operations and apprehend it.

J. J. What is the difference between the two prayers?

J. T. Well, the first refers to the "eyes of your heart"; it is more the intelligence, the "spirit of wisdom and revelation". This is but little understood, but what we had here last night as to divine appearings ought to help us as to it. You have the principle in Peter the prototype of Christians in relation to the church: "flesh and blood has not revealed it to thee, but my Father who is

in the heavens" (Matt. xvi. 17). Of course
in his case it was special, but the principle
is found in this epistle, the "spirit of wisdom
and revelation"; it comes from God; it comes
by prayer. It is not a question of ministry,
but of prayer; it is directly from God. So,
here, the strengthening of the inner man comes
by prayer, from the Father.

C. O. B.   Does the expression "the inner
man" indicate formation in the saints?

J. T.   I think it does. It is not what people
see, but what relates to God, though it has
an effect outwardly, of course.

A. E. M.   Does this prayer bring in the
thought of the work of God as a complete
answer to His counsels?

J. T.   Well, I think it does, giving ability
to take in divine things: "that ye may be
fully able to apprehend with all the saints
what is the breadth and length and depth
and height". The "inner man" includes the
automatic organs of the man, so that he is
able, as such, to stand in the midst of the
great divine sphere and apprehend it. I do
not believe one could do this mentally; it is
a question of ability in the inner man, all the
automatic organs being in action.

G. W. W.   What do you mean by the automatic organs?

J. T. They are alluded to in scripture, the organs that you cannot adjust or affect by the action of your mind. The Spirit operates through these organs, as well as the mind. They are referred to in the word "reins" in the Psalms and other Scriptures.

The Lord alludes to them in John iv. Water refers to that part of the body more than breath. Breath is for the lungs. The believer becomes alive, not only mentally, but in all his being. He is living and energetic inwardly.

QUES. Is this what is referred to in Leviticus?

J. T. I think so; the inward parts are laid out before God on the altar.

E. R. What about the "riches of his glory"?

J. T. In chapter i. He is the "Father of glory"; He is the source of it, but here it is the "riches of his glory". The riches of the Father's glory is a very wonderful thought. "The God of glory" appeared to Abraham, and I suppose that enters into the working out of His thoughts; now we have the glory itself, so that the assembly according to this chapter, becomes the residence of it: "To him be glory in the assembly in Christ Jesus unto all generations of the age of ages". That is what the apostle has in view, and I think one of the most beautiful touches in the chapter is the note of worship from him here. He says, "But to him that is able to do far exceedingly above all which we ask or think, according to the power which works in us, to him be glory in the assembly in Christ Jesus unto all generations of the age of ages. Amen". That is the end of the parenthesis, including almost the whole chapter; and what a parenthesis it is! What wealth is in it, ending with this note of worship!

QUES. Would you say a word as to the measurements? There are four here; in the heavenly city there are only three.

J. T. The fourth dimension is remarkable. I do not know much about dimensions, but "the depth" seems to bring in the death of Christ. I suppose in ordinary things there are only three dimensions, but the death of Christ, I think, brings in the fourth, the depth to which He went.

God is the "God of measure", and it must enter into creation, but I think the fourth dimension alludes to the love that led Christ down into the depths.

M. W. B. What do you understand by the expression here, "that ye may be filled even to all the fulness of God"?

J. T. Well, according to what we had yesterday, that is eternity. That is what I understand. We are filled into what is infinitely beyond us—not lost in it; I am intelligently in it. It is not in God exactly, but to "the fulness", which would mean the shining out of Himself in Christ.

IV

READING

A. M. H. Would you mind saying how far the last verse of chapter iii. goes? "Unto all generations of the age of ages".

J. T. I have taken it to be in keeping with similar expressions in the epistle, such as "eternal purpose". Then you have in chapter iii. 9, "throughout the ages", referring to what is past; then again, the "purpose of the ages" (verse 11). I regard the verse you mention as meaning eternity in the future.

A. M. H. I was wondering whether it would be the result of the dip of which you have spoken. God is now bringing into eternity what is suitable to eternity.

J. T. That is what I thought; He will have something now in the eternity to come, that He did not have in the past. The idea would correspond with the end of Psalm cvi. to which allusion has been made, which David included in his psalm as the ark was brought to Zion: "Blessed be Jehovah the God of

Israel, from eternity to eternity". It seems
as if the apostle is in keeping with that in this
remark. It is a beautiful note of worship,
because it rises to the full height of what is
presented. The expression in chapter i., "the
administration of the fulness of times", is
more limited and describes the culmination
in the coming age of the various testimonies
rendered, but this verse, being the outburst
of his feelings in worship, goes to the full length
of the thought of God. It is what accrues to
Him in the assembly in eternity.

H. D'A. C. The "administration of the
fulness of times" refers to the millennial period,
does it not?

J. T. Yes, I thought so. The phrase translated "all generations of the age of ages"
in chapter iii. 21 implies eternity. Our minds
can hardly go any further than what is conveyed in that expression.

F. H. B. The expression used here is the
strongest for eternity.

J. T. When you have "times", you are
within the sphere of testimony. Times and
seasons are governed by the heavenly bodies,
but "eternity to eternity" is descriptive of
God Himself, and implies that which is beyond
a provisional condition of things in the heavens
and earth. So that being "filled even to all

the fulness of God" would suggest what is in view.

J. J. Would it be like the verse in 1 Corinthians xv. "Then the Son also himself shall be placed in subjection to him who put all things in subjection to him, that God may be all in all"?

J. T. That is the line of thought. The fulness of God is the end here; we are to be filled to all the fulness of God. We are in fixedness, not lost in infinitude. We are in infinitude, but fixed in it intelligently, as I may say. "The fulness of God" refers to what has shone out in Christ.

A. M. H. What would be the force of "generations" in that verse; "unto all generations"?

J. T. I suppose it is what springs from God. The idea of generation is different from creation. I think it brings in the divine parentage of every family in the heavens and the earth. The whole epistle has God in view as the source of all.

G. W. W. Why does it say, "Age of ages"?

J. T. I do not understand it very much. It is an intensive thought conveying eternity.

H. H. The "Father of whom every family . . . is named" would correspond with what you have said about generation.

· J. T. I think so. The two ideas of generation and creation run together, but generation,
involves the nature of God.

F. H. B. Is that more connected with John's
writings?

J. T. I think it is.

F. H. B. And "new creation" more connected with Paul.

J. T. Well, of course John has the new
creation and Paul speaks of the family, but
I think that generation is more John's line.
In his 1st chapter we have it: "who have
been born, not of blood nor of flesh's will nor
of man's will, but of God" (verse 13). It
brings us into correspondence with Christ as
Son.

QUES. Could you help us on the thought
of families? Chapter iii. speaks of "every
family" in the heavens and on the earth.
Which families would come to your mind in
thinking of that?

J. T. I have no doubt that families are
formed according to testimonies rendered.
Besides angels and the church there will be
families in heaven. There will also be families
on the earth out of Israel and the nations.
You have "*all* generations". They are generations that spring from God. It is really a higher
thought, and brings us more into relation with

Christ, than the idea of creation. He is the beginning of the creation, but no part of it, but the idea of generation is attached to Christ; He is the Son of God, and the Son of David.

A. M. H. The assembly is really the central body and conveys all the thoughts of God.

P. L. Would you connect the tabernacle of God in the eternal state as with men, with the different families?

J. T. The word "men" would cover them all, though I suppose angels might come in. The tabernacle is distinct of course. It is a very wonderful thought that the apostle should bring it in in a note of worship. He is so absorbed by the depths of the things of which he is speaking, that he breaks out into this wonderful note as to what God would have "in the assembly in Christ Jesus unto all generations of the age of ages". There can be no doubt that, whilst chapter iii. is parenthetical, it is to effect what we have here in chapter iv., namely, the unity that is befitting to us, the "unity of the Spirit" (verse 3) and the "unity of the faith" (verse 13). The Lord may help us under those two heads, and then the self-action in the upbuilding of the body.

A. S. L. Is it not one of those passages where the apostle is so overpowered with the infinite greatness of what he is expressing, that he, as it were, coins phrases and terms? As, for instance, not content to say the "least of all saints" he says, "less than the least". It is that kind of thing. So, "unto all generations of the age of ages" is surely his way of giving some idea of eternity.

J. T. The epistle is full of intensified expressions. We want to go the whole way, which is the principle of Ephesians; unity here is on the same principle. It is based on the full revelation of God, the three Persons being included in verses 4 and 6.

A. S. L. This morning there was a word on the "prisoner of Christ Jesus".

J. T. In chapter iii. it is the "prisoner of Christ Jesus", but here it is "in the Lord". The first is that Christ had imprisoned him; in the second it is perfectly evident he is not a felon; it was apparent to all that his bonds were "in Christ" (Phil. i. 13). Here, he is "prisoner in the Lord".

F. H. B. In connection with the unity of the Spirit, are there not three circles?

J. T. "One body and one Spirit, as ye have been also called in one hope of your calling;" "one Lord, one faith, one baptism;"

"one God and Father of all, who is over all, and through all, and in us all". So that the unity is really connected with the three Persons of the Godhead, as already said.

A. S. L. Then, would "with all lowliness and meekness, with long-suffering" be something of the character of Peter's shadow and the virtue from Paul, of which you were speaking?

J. T. Just so. The "prisoner in the Lord" is enjoining this. "I . . . exhort you therefore to walk worthy of the calling wherewith ye have been called, with all lowliness and meekness, with long-suffering, bearing with one another in love; using diligence to keep the unity of the Spirit in the uniting bond of peace."

A. S. L. That would be the character of those in whom the unity is seen.

J. T. It involves smallness, in keeping with the manner of divine revelation; it is in smallness here. Otherwise we shall have a lot of extraneous matter in the unity. If it be a unity in which anything of the flesh has any place, there will be extraneous matter that God will have to grind out through discipline. Here we are instructed as to how to avoid that,—"with all lowliness and meekness".

A. S. L. These are the traits of the "new man" he speaks of later.

J. T. They would be, only that the new man is more public, more for testimony. This has to do with our relations with one another; "bearing with one another in love".

J. J. Why is it called the "unity of the Spirit"?

J. T. It is the full thought, in keeping with this epistle. There is nothing less than that in the mind of God. It means that we are linked up in spiritual affection. The gold taches of the tabernacle typify this unity; we are linked up definitely in the unity of the Spirit. It is positive.

A. S. L. We have to use diligence to keep that.

J. T. It was already there and the Ephesians were to keep it in the way prescribed here.

A. S. L. Then "there is one body" is a definite statement; no case of endeavouring to set up another.

J. T. The three-fold unity that follows is brought in as affording an intelligent basis for the end to which we are moving. God has come down as we see. Revelation involves the unity of the Godhead, the Father, the Son and the Spirit, so that the basis is no less than that. That is what the epistle teaches. It is to maintain us in the height of the revelation of God, this entering into our relations with one another. So the platform is very great and grand, and each one, however obscure, is to move in that light. He sees that the revelation of God involves unity in outward smallness. The Lord Jesus came here in that manner.

A. S. L. What is the idea of the unity of the Spirit?

J. T. As we were saying, it is a question of the brethren being formed in spiritual affections, so that there are practical links with one another. The "unity of the faith" is a matter of our thinking the same thing and speaking the same thing, holding in our souls the truth unitedly; but the "unity of the Spirit" refers to what the Spirit promotes, including, as we have been saying, what is suggested by the lower organs of man as well as the intelligence, for faith necessarily has to do with the intelligence,—what I believe. But the unity of the Spirit goes beyond that, and involves the work of the Holy Ghost in the whole man, so that there are affections in which we are linked together. We have all been "made to drink into one Spirit".

H. H. Do you think Psalms cxxxii. and cxxxiii. correspond in some respects with

chapters iii. and iv.? Christ dwelling in the
heart by faith corresponding with the thought
of the ark coming into its resting place, and
then the result in the unity seen in this chapter.

J. T. I think that is right; the symbols of
unity in Psalm cxxxiii. allude to the Spirit.

H. H. There is the suggestion of a past
history in relation to the matter. The tribes
had not been moving together in unity.

J. T. In his great apprehension of it,
David brought the ark to Zion. The time it
was at Kirjath-jearim "was long", it says, "for
it was twenty years" (1 Sam. vii. 2). That,
I apprehend, was from the time that it was
taken, until Samuel's ministry began. The
people lamented after Jehovah and this was
morally giving the ark its place. David's
literal restoration of the ark was the culmination of that movement. The first feature of
the restoration was seen when the people of
Israel poured out water before the Lord
(1 Sam. vii. 6.) which was a remarkable
expression of self abnegation, the confession
of what we are. The pouring out water
here is not as the wise woman of Tekoah
said, "We . . . are as water spilt on the
ground, which cannot be gathered up again".
Samuel does not say that of the people under
his ministry. They poured water out *before*

G

the Lord, and that is another matter. What
is impossible with man is possible with God;
the water poured out on the ground before the
Lord, can be gathered up again figuratively
speaking. And then Samuel offers a sucking
lamb, "a whole burnt-offering" which presents
a *whole* idea. I think this chapter (1 Sam. vii.)
would promote that, but beginning with that
abject state in the soul that God can recognize.
David's movement follows morally, and so the
ark was brought to Zion. There you have
the idea of a centre of unity; so that when
David had to flee from Jerusalem on account
of Absalom, going up the hill of Olivet, Zadok
and the Levites with him brought the ark,
as if the centre could be transferred. But we
cannot transfer the centre of unity, any more
than we can transfer the centre of gravity.
God has set it up Himself and it is set up
for ever; it is in Zion, so the ark remains
there. David said, "Carry back the ark of
God into the city"; he was not going to make
another centre. There is a danger of that,
thinking we can transfer the centre of unity,
but you cannot do that; it would spoil the
whole moral system if it could be done by
man, but it cannot. God has set it up, and
everything revolves around the centre. "I, if
I be lifted up out of the earth, will draw all

to me", He says (John xii. 32). The ark was only a symbol, but rightly understood it was the glory. That is to say, it was God come in, in the lowliest circumstances. It was His glory and it was His power, so that we need not be afraid of smallness according to God. The glory and power of God were bound up with the ark. Whenever it moved in the wilderness the enemies were scattered. When David brought it to Zion it was installed according to divine purpose; it had reached its rest typically.

W. R. P. Bringing the ark into the camp was making a new centre, and then David's action was the answer to that in faith.

J. T. Quite; he leaves it in its proper place, and, in fleeing before Absalom, said, "If I shall find favour in the eyes of Jehovah, he will bring me again, and shew me it, and its habitation". So that we need not be afraid of smallness; it is God's way in testimony. Largeness according to God belongs to the past eternity, and the coming one will also be large. We shall be fixed in it there, according to chapter iii., but the point now is smallness. Smallness according to God means invulnerability; nothing can stand before it. So David says, "Carry back the ark of God into the city", and there it was during Absalom's time. It meant the over-throw of Absalom, because along with the ark there was a system set up by David in secrecy within the city, that meant the over-throw of Absalom's system. Thus David came back to the ark and its habitation. Hence Psalm cxxxiii. rightly follows Psalm cxxxii. In the latter Psalm, the afflictions of David are spoken of and how he had heard of the ark and found it. "We heard of it at Ephratah", he says, and "we found it in the fields of the wood". Then, "I will not give sleep to mine eyes, slumber to mine eyelids, until I find out a place for Jehovah, habitations for the Mighty One of Jacob". You feel that unity in that connection is fixed, that we are moving in a unity that will never be broken up.

M. W. B. You spoke just now of a secret system in connection with the ark which in-volved the overthrow of Absalom. Would that apply to the unity of the Spirit? Is that a system that implies the overthrow of the whole world's system?

J. T. I think so. There were old and young brothers left behind in Jerusalem, (see 2 Sam. xv.) and if there had not been the unity of the Spirit, they would have been discerned. It was not the time to say much because talkativeness would have exposed them and

what they were set for. It was a question of
the unity of the Spirit, old brothers and young
brothers being there; and then a little maid
is brought into it, and then a well, and corn
placed over the well's mouth by a woman
to hide the messengers. All these things are
typical of the unity of the Spirit. It was a
very obscure thing, but it meant the overthrow of Absalom's system, and the return
of David to the ark and its habitation.

M. W. B. What relation has the walking
worthy of the calling with that? We are to
"walk worthy of the calling wherewith ye
have been called with all lowliness and meekness". Does that refer back to the end
of chapter ii. or the beginning of chapter i.?

J. T. I should include all that is said about
us in chapters i. and ii. Whenever you have
anything in Ephesians, you have the fulness
of it. It is not being called into the fellowship of God's Son, etc., as in Corinthians,
which involves being called out of the world,
as does the calling referred to in 1 Corinthians
i. 26; so, too, called "out of darkness" in
1 Pet. ii. 9. Here in Ephesians it is the
greatness of the calling in its full and positive
character.

J. J. It is said of brethren dwelling together in unity that it is "like the precious

oil upon the head, that ran down upon the beard, upon Aaron's beard, that ran down to the hem of his garments" (Psa. cxxxiii. 2). What is the idea of running down?

J. T. I have no doubt you begin with the idea of headship, the head of Aaron, and then the beard would be his appearance. That is, it brings in the Person of the Lord in His priestly position. Then you have the "dew of Hermon," the link between heaven and earth. The ointment flowing down involves the headship of Christ, and the beard the appearance, and the skirts of His garments would be the saints all linked up with Him.

QUES. Is the unity essential to eternal life, for it says, "There the Lord commanded the blessing, even life for evermore"?

J. T. It is in Psalm cxxxiii., but we are on higher ground here in Ephesians. We are not dealing in this chapter with eternal life, but with the church and the unity that is proper to it, so that we reach what might be termed a self-acting feature; the body acts of itself (Eph. iv. 16).

G. W. W. Are we to learn anything in the incident of the ark being mentioned at the moment of Jonathan's victory over the Philistines? It is said, "The ark of God was at that time with the children of Israel" (1 Sam.

xiv. 18). I was thinking of what you said as to smallness and the victory. Things had got to a very low level at that time, but Jonathan in the faith of his soul was in the good of what was indicated in the ark —"Rise up, Lord, and let thine enemies be scattered".

J. T. It is a very interesting connection as corresponding with 2 Samuel xv. and entering into this chapter, because the unity here referred to is not a question of what we are *saying* but of inwardly understanding one another. In the case of Jonathan and his armour bearer, they had to keep very quiet, and the secrecy was effective.

J. H. T. Do you get that kind of unity with Paul and his last contact with the Ephesian elders? It says that he "prayed with them all. And they all wept sore; and falling upon the neck of Paul they ardently kissed him".

J. T. I think so. Notice, they fell upon "the *neck* of Paul". That would mean much, as to what he had staked. The unity of the Spirit is not exactly what is spoken, but involves a subtle relation with each other that cannot be overthrown. We understand one another; the thing is there.

QUES. Would Philippians ii. enter into it, showing that the whole man is involved?

"If then there be any comfort in Christ, if any consolation of love, if any fellowship of the Spirit, if any bowels and compassions, fulfil my joy, that ye may think the same thing, having the same love, joined in soul, thinking one thing".

J. T. Exactly. There is not a word spoken. It is inward correspondence.

M. W. B. Do you link the unity of the Spirit rather with the inner man of chapter iii. and the unity of the faith with the prayer of chapter i.?

J. T. Yes; that is a very good distinction. I believe that the unity of the Spirit is the invulnerable thing. It means that we are invulnerable, that we are bound to go through, as we were saying about the ark and David sending it back. He knew it was the centre but there was alongside it, that which very aptly illustrates this unity of the Spirit in Hushai, Zadok and the others with them who were with the ark in the city, and their success depended on maintaining that unity. They inwardly corresponded with one another; they felt together and moved in unity.

H. H. One thinks of it in connection with church difficulties. Do you think that this scripture. "Using diligence to keep the unity of the Spirit in the uniting bond of peace" would mean that so far as we have light and our brethren with us have light, we should seek to move in line with what is fully consistent with the revelation of God as set out in this epistle? We cannot make others agree with us; often difficulties arise; but should we not seek to be governed by the light that has come from the Lord and which is supported by the Spirit?

J. T. Yes, but I think it is well to bear in mind that this unity as has just been remarked, is more that of the inward man, meaning that we are linked up together in a sort of subtle, or inward way, so that if you go to the care meeting, for example, that principle of unity is there.

M. W. B. It would govern us in relation to one another.

J. T. You would bear in mind that it must not be interfered with; it is better to leave things over than that *that* should be interfered with. It is a thing that God intends should exist, and it means invulnerability as far as we are concerned.

H. H. Nobody could ever break that down.

J. T. Here, too, it is rather the responsibility to keep it, that is referred to, and the way it is to be done is "with all lowliness and meekness, with long-suffering, bearing with

one another in love; using diligence to keep
the unity of the Spirit in the uniting bond
of peace". That is the first thing to bear
in mind if you go to a care meeting. I do
not mean to say that any principles have to
be made secondary, but it is better to leave
things over for another time than to break
in on this. It is imperative, and if brethren
do not agree in one matter they may be able
to in some other matter; this helps to maintain the unity (Comp. Phil. iii. 15, 16).

J. O. S. Do we see in Paul's letter to
Philemon his endeavouring to keep the unity
of the Spirit?

J. T. We do indeed. It was written with
very great wisdom and patience, without any
expression of authority. There are times when
we would wisely avoid alluding to any advantage we may have. It may be we want to
get a "brother beloved" reinstated. The
apostle refers to his age rather than to his
apostleship, but mark, not his age by itself; he
did not mention how many years old he was.
It is not that, because I may be a hundred and
not have any moral weight. He said, "being
such a one as Paul the aged"—*that* aged man.

QUES. How would you speak of unity
without agreement? You spoke of letting
things stand over.

J. T. Agreement must be founded on unity. The unity exists, but if you cannot agree, the matter may be left over, and no ground lost.

REM. I take it, if we find ourselves not in agreement, that ought to be a matter of great concern in view of the unity of the Spirit existing as you say, and which is available to us on a practical line in regard to any question which may arise.

J. T. I think if the unity of the Spirit is maintained agreement will come, but it may take time; the apostle has that in view when he speaks about "all lowliness and meekness, with long-suffering, bearing with one another in love; using diligence". It involves much concern and earnestness.

P. L. Do you get the idea in Acts xxi.? "And when he would not be persuaded, we were silent, saying, The will of the Lord be done."

J. T. Very good. They might have quarrelled with Paul, urging how wrong it was to go up to Jerusalem, but they were too much in the unity of the Spirit for that.

S. J. B. C. Can the unity of the Spirit be broken?

J. T. It says "to keep" it. Abstractly it is fixed and eternal.

J. J. What link has the unity of the Spirit with the body? The passage goes on to speak of the body, so there would seem to be some very intimate link.

J. T. Surely. There are the three circles as was remarked; the first connected with the Spirit, "one body and one Spirit, as ye have been also called in one hope of your calling"; that is the inner thing. The next is the unity connected with the Lord: "one Lord, one faith, one baptism"; that is a wider circle, as has often been remarked. Then you have "one God and Father of all, who is over all, and through all, and in us all"; that goes to infinitude.

D. L. H. Are there not three concentric circles spoken of here and the Spirit the centre controlling all three?

J. T. I should say that. The unity of the Spirit would enter into all three; that is, it runs through whatever you are dealing with, the secret relations with one another run right through; you never give that up.

E. S. H. Divine principles are to be maintained, but it is a question of *how* you maintain them.

J. T. Yes; there is something peculiarly fine in the unity of the Spirit; it implies the affections being in action.

QUES. Why does it say, "one God and Father of all", not Christ or the Lord?

J. T. I think it is to bring in the universal idea. The Father is in the supreme place of Godhead and the circle in that connection is widest. Hence one *God* and Father.

A. S. L. How far does "all" go?

J. T. It is universal, but refers only to Christians.

D. L. H. Has that not a reference to the end of chapter iii.? "Of whom every family in the heavens and on earth is named".

J. T. The apostle is dealing with the present position, the unity of Christians, so he brings it down to "over all, and through all, and in *us* all" limiting the idea in the last clause. I suppose the expression does involve the supremacy of God as the Father in the whole created sphere, but the apostle limits the bearing of it to Christians, those in whom the Father is.

F. H. B. Does not this agree with what will be brought to pass in the eternal state? It will be seen then that there is "one God and Father of all" and all will recognize Him in that way.

J. T. God will then be "all in all" (1 Cor. xv. 28).

G. W. W. Do you think the unity of the Spirit in this wide universal aspect has any connection with what the Lord said, that "he is good to the unthankful and wicked" (Luke vi. 35)? That is the attitude of God towards men generally which has to be maintained by the saints at the present time.

J. T.   I am sure that should enter into our exercises as in the unity of the Spirit.

After this we enter on the subject of gift. "But to each one of us has been given grace according to the measure of the gift of the Christ".

H. H.   Would you mind explaining that verse?

J. T.   It is grace for service. John says, "of his fulness we all have received, and grace upon grace". In that passage it is not measure; it seems to be one wave after another coming to you; He gives more and more. But here in Ephesians it is measure, as if the Lord in giving, takes account of the vessel, for each vessel is capable of a certain thing and He knows the measure: "according to the measure of the gift of the Christ".

F. H. B.   Is all this about gift connected with the proper working of the body?

J. T.   I think you come to that in verse 16 where you have the joints and bands which are the outcome of this. The human body is another figure that the apostle uses. But

first the principle of giving, as we have it
here, is according to measure, and the measure
must be in relation to the person to whom
the gift is given.

QUES. Is the measure seen in the bowl
full of water? (Judges vi. 38).

J. T. Just so. The vessel was full.

REM. The grace is commensurate with the
gift.

J. T. The gift here *is* the grace. The first
reference here is not a specific gift such as
an apostle; it is a question of what everybody
gets. Every one of us gets something, but it
is according to the "measure of the gift of
the Christ". It is His measure and He would
take account of what you can use.

QUES. What about the measure of faith in
Romans?

J. T. It is the same idea. "As God has
dealt to each a measure of faith" (Rom. xii.
3). Romans of course is the initial thing, and
faith is necessary, but here it is grace. Then
he goes on to speak about Christ ascended.
The One who gives the gifts, who is He? The
same One that "descended into the lower
parts of the earth", and He has "also ascended
up above all the heavens, that he might fill
all things". Well now, He is going to fill
me. But then He gives gifts unto *men*; that

is not to everybody. We are coming now to something distinctive and specific, because the specific gifts are to men.

J. R. S. Why is it "far above all heavens" in connection with giving gifts?

J. T. I think to show the supremacy of Christ's power; He has "ascended up above all the heavens", so that the gift being received from Him there, means that I have something that no power in the universe can overthrow. You will find in 1 Chronicles that when David is anointed, the names of the mighties are given at once, because it is a question of what they will do for him. In 2 Samuel they are given at the end of his reign. 2 Samuel would indicate that the gifts come down to the end and that all are included in the record.

In this second part of the scripture (verses 8–14) the apostle is not dealing with what is general to believers, as in verse 7, but with what is specific. These gifts are not contemplated as being given to what is immature; he is not dealing with children. Every believer receives something from Christ, but when you come to these great powers from "above all the heavens" it is men that are in view. Not men who make playthings of them but who will use them for Christ, as the "three" broke through the camp of the Philistines and drew water for David. That is the sort of service that these gifts are for, so that Christ may have in the assembly a full result. "For the perfecting of the saints; with a view to the work of the ministry, with a view to the edifying of the body of Christ".

J. J. As the apostles are put first in the list here, would they belong to the first category of the mighties, the mightiest?

J. T. I think they are in the order of wisdom. The apostle brings in authority; he establishes his testimony in authority, and the prophet shows that the mind of God is in it, that it is not of man, but the mind of God. The evangelist is to make God known through the gospel, to secure material for the assembly; and the pastor and teacher is to adjust the minds of the saints by teaching. The order is authority, the mind of God, the heart of God, and then the adjustment by teaching.

F. H. B. The teacher and pastor seem to be identified together.

J. T. That is how it stands; it is one gift. The teacher instructs the saints in power. As pastor he looks after the sheep.

REM. It says, "until we all arrive".

J. T. "All" is put there; this is characteristic of Ephesians.

H

H. D'A. C.   Is not maturity the point here
—that we are not to be children? Pastors
may have to give their lives for the sheep.

J. T.   Was not that spirit with David when
he took the lamb out of the lion's mouth?
He rescued the lamb; he did not merely take
out a pair of legs or a piece of an ear, but he
secured the *whole* lamb and slew the lion and
the bear; he put himself in jeopardy for the
flock.

QUES.   What is the thought of leading
captivity captive?

J. T.   I think Goliath's head is the symbol
of it. David took the head of Goliath to
Jerusalem, answering to "having ascended up
on high". In the type, I think, Jerusalem is
on high; it is the place of power, and then,
I believe, the mighties are the gifts, and what
wonderful men they were!

A. S. L.   Would you say one word on the
remarkable expression, "the measure of the
stature of the fulness of the Christ"?

.J. T.   I think it refers to the gospels. That
is where you get the "measure of the stature
of the fulness of the Christ". This epistle is
very near to the elevation of the gospels.

J. J.   Especially John?

J. T.   All of them, Each one presents some
feature of Christ,

A. S. L. So you think the "measure of the stature of the fulness of the Christ" is what is set forth in the four gospels?

J. T. Yes. So in each of the four gospels the Lord has need in regard of what we are speaking of: "The Lord has need of it". I do not mean that in each of the gospels that is stated. In Matthew He has need of *them*, but it would be in relation to Matthew's presentation of Christ. The need of the Lord would be in that relation. There were two there, an ass and a colt. The Lord has need of those for the assembly, to set up new meetings. That is what Matthew would promote; He has need of the two, the old and the young brother. But in Mark it is one colt which would be in relation to the ministry, the preaching; He has need of preachers. Then in Luke He has need of priests, persons that can pray. In John He finds the colt *Himself*. He does not use the disciples to find it. I think this is the position now. He indicates that He can get one Himself and get on without us; but in each of the synoptic gospels He uses two disciples.

F. H. B. Is the general thought in this scripture that the Lord has made adequate provision for carrying the testimony through according to His own mind?

J. T. That is so; hence you come to full growth, and that is the "measure of the stature of the fulness of the Christ".

H. D'A. C. Each one must come to that.

J. T. "Until we *all* arrive". The fulness of Christ is what has come out in Him. It is not a question of His Deity, but what has shone out in Him as a Man.

A. S. L. Would it connect at all with chapter i.? "The assembly, which is his body, the fulness of him who fills all in all".

J. T. That is the church. The church is His fulness as His body, but this fulness is what has shone out in Christ in His ways and ministry, seen in the gospels, as a standard for each of us. It has all in view however.

V

READING

EPHESIANS V. 22–33.

J. T. There are two main subjects in the chapters still to be considered—the church and the conflict; we might concentrate on these. It was thought that the details in the exhortatory part of chapters iv. and v. might be left as time does not permit of going into them. The assembly in a peculiar way is brought to our attention in the verses read, and this affords an opportunity for briefly looking into the whole subject. There are, however, two features in chapters iv. and v. that might first be touched upon; namely, the "new man" in chapter iv. and the "beloved children" in chapter v. On those two features hang, practically, all that is said in detail, the "new man" having reference to what we put on, being more public; and the subject of "beloved children" bringing us into very close correspondence with Christ. Certain conduct is treated as hinging on these two features.

Then another point in chapter iv. is the "unity of the faith" which was scarcely noticed yesterday. We were engaged generally with the "unity of the Spirit"; but the "unity of the faith" as having a bearing upon full growth, is a very important matter in its setting in chapter iv. leading up to the self-action of the body, which implies the absence of the babe condition (verses 1–16) and involves each being in his place in intelligence and affection. The chapter speaks of both the unity of the Spirit and the unity of the faith, the latter implying that those who compose the assembly should never assume that there *must* be differences existing. The saints being fully grown should surely be able, in the presence of the Lord, to see the right and wrong of everything. I thought it would be well, perhaps, to mention these general features in chapter iv. and the early part of chapter v., before we take up our definite subject which is the assembly.

N. McC. Do you connect the unity of the faith more with intelligence than affection?

J. T. Yes. The unity of the Spirit, as we had yesterday, is properly linked up with the affections. The unity of the faith having reference to our minds, our intelligence; but it is not simply a matter of doctrine, as I understand, but what is *held in faith*. Christianity is not a system of doctrines; there are doctrines, but it is a question of what is held in faith, therefore it is called "the faith".

M. W. B. Is that why the unity of the faith is linked with the knowledge of the Son of God?

J. T. Yes; the Son of God, in the passage, refers to what He is on God's side, and the "measure of the stature of the fulness of the Christ" is what He is on our side.

J. J. Would there be a connection between the "one new man" of chapter ii., the "inner man" of chapter iii., and the "full-grown man" and the "new man" of chapter iv.?

J. T. I think there is an interesting link in those passages.

J. J. How would that bear on the assembly? I suppose it is material for it.

J. T. It leads up to it. The assembly is found in each of the chapters up to this one. In chapter i. it is spoken of as the fulness of Christ; in chapter ii. as the habitation of God; then twice in chapter iii., first as that in which the all-various wisdom of God is seen by the principalities and powers in the heavenlies, and then as the vessel of divine glory in eternity; then in chapter iv. it is referred to as the body and as self-edifying here, the saints set together in full growth so that there is self-acting. It is an organism in which all the members are in their places.

Eu. R. We have looked too much at this thought of full growth as being future, and that to which we are moving on.

J. T. I think it is clearly present, with a view to the increase of the body, to its self-building up in love. You find the church in each of these chapters up to this one; we have a greater view of the church here than in any other epistle. Above all subjects a knowledge of the types is essential to a right understanding of the church as presented in this epistle. In Genesis we have three types. There are others, but the principal ones are Eve, Rebecca and Asnath. In the wilderness we have Zipporah and the Ethiopian (wives of Moses); then in Joshua we have Achsah; and in 1 Samuel we have Abigail. There are other types in a lesser way, but I think these are the great types. The first, Eve, is really the greatest type, as I understand it, because it is a type of the church viewed apart from sin, and was given before sin came in. All the others contemplate the existence of the moral question, but Eve is the church viewed apart from sin, and was a type given before the moral issue was raised, and therefore she sets forth the idea of "from eternity to eternity", so to speak. "Eternity to eternity" would mean that the church in the coming eternity has no reference to a past sinful history at all. It has a life out of death; not death as penalty, but death illustrated in sleep and as expressive of love. Then Rebecca would be the church as *brought to* Christ, being of equal family dignity, to replace Israel; Asnath would be the church as seen in Colossians—Christ among the Gentiles; then Zipporah and the Ethiopian viewed together, would be the church in the wilderness, suggesting peculiarly, Corinthians. Achsah is the church viewed as laying hold of the inheritance, valuing and appreciating it; and finally Abigail is the church militant. I mention all these, because I think they enter into the subject before us, as essential to a right understanding of it.

W. J. H. In what way would you connect the church as "from eternity"?

J. T. Well, Eve coming in before sin, indicates what was in the mind or purpose of God. She was needed; it was not good that man should be alone; and she is brought in for Adam before sin came in. That is, Eve would represent purpose. But by way of contrast, you cannot think of Zipporah in the same way, nor the Ethiopian woman who was a sort of counterpart to Zipporah. Those types suggest wilderness features. What is said of them is brief and would indicate there was nothing attractive. Of the church in the wilderness you cannot say much; it is a question of what it proves itself to be, but it is there.

Eu. R. Is your suggestion that Eve illustrates the assembly as wholly spiritual?

J. T. Quite so, as taken out of Christ. You cannot apply that to Zipporah. Adam says, "This time it is bone of my bones and flesh of my flesh". Eve is the church as entirely spiritual, and as we have it in its highest feature in this epistle.

J. J. Would not that be seen in the first six verses of chapter i.?

J. T. Yes, and in the beginning of chapter ii. It includes union; we are quickened *with the Christ.*

QUES. Would Eve as a type suggest to us the manifold wisdom you spoke about yesterday morning?

J. T. Well, I do not know that you could limit that to this type. What the saints are down here *now* is alluded to there: "in order that now to the principalities and authorities in the heavenlies might be made known through the assembly the all-various wisdom of God". I think the idea of the church as typified in Eve, in an abstract way runs through this dispensation, to shew what was in the mind of God from eternity, and the church as seen in her—goes into eternity.

F. H. B. It is important to see that what God is doing now, is not merely with a view to meeting man's need, but to carry out what was in His mind for eternity, for His own pleasure—the building of the woman.

J. T. That is what I had in mind. Eve is the greatest type, I think, and, as we were saying about the basket, she must be understood as abstractly existing. There is, however, very little known amongst us of the concrete idea of the church seen in this type. But she is there; the thread runs right through. She is out of Christ, not as having died under penalty, but in the character of sleep, so that the moral question does not enter into it. That comes in later, and enters into the fibre of the church. The fibre gives lustre; but Eve is the church of purpose, to which we come when we are clear in our souls of all that refers to the moral issue.

QUES. If no sin is attached to Eve as "from eternity", in what way does the cleansing come in here in chapter v., the "washing of water"?

J. T. You cannot limit these verses to that type. The type is alluded to, but the church is presented here in other relations besides.

The subject comes in here as confirming the apostle's instruction as to wives.

C. A. C.   Would you say it was the thought of God that the Eve character of the assembly should come into concrete evidence now, and would the cleansing have that in view?

J. T.   I think the cleansing frees us, so that we might enter into what the church is in purpose. Was not that the great burden of the ministry of J. B. S.—to bring us to apprehend that the church has come out of Christ, and that all that goes to heaven comes out of heaven?

A. E. M.   Would the Eve type be suggested in John xx. where the Lord showed them His hands and His side?

J. T.   I think that is right; it fits properly there because it is the chapter in which the first day of the week is in evidence; it is mentioned twice. His *side*, alluding to Adam, is the link, I think. The first day of the week being emphasised in John is important. It is not the day after the Sabbath; it is the first day. John has in view, not a development from the ways of God in the Old Testament, but a wholly new thing, the "first" having no reference to anything earlier. Rightly understood, it would therefore suggest the entrance into what is of eternity; that is what is there. The church has come in that way, from the side of Christ. The fact that it is not formally mentioned does not affect the general idea conveyed in the chapter.

M. W. B. With reference to sleep or death do you think it would help us as to the supper, —the Lord's love seen apart from penalty?

J. T. I think that is right. John's gospel hardly presents the death of Christ as penalty. There is no forsaking—nor is there in Luke. Not, of course, that it is not there; but the truth is presented in John's gospel from a different side.

Eu. R. Is Matthew xvi. the Eve character? "I will build my assembly".

J. T. Somewhat, but I think that includes Abigail, that is, the church militant—"hades' gates shall not prevail against it".

A. M. H. Would you connect the thought of His flesh with the character of man in Luke, and His bones with the order of man in John?

J. T. John it is that speaks about the bones being unbroken. John refers to flesh too. I think John makes more of the flesh of Christ than any of the evangelists. "The Word became flesh" in chapter i. and in chapter vi. he makes a great deal of it. The food in John is His flesh, but the food in Matthew and Mark is the *body* of Christ.

J. H. B. What is the difference between the flesh of Christ and His body?

J. T. The flesh is *condition*, but the body conveys a *whole* idea and suggests unity. I think this is what is prominent in the synoptic gospels. The church is reached there more from the standpoint of the wilderness, and the Lord's body is spoken of so that we should have a whole idea. We come into the assembly in connection with the body as presented in the Lord's supper, which we do not get in John. The body is to present the church as a whole idea, a complete thought, as answering to a complete thought in Christ; so that the food in Matthew and Mark is His body: "Take, eat: this is my body". But in John, the eating is the flesh, that we might be imbued or built up in a constitution answering to the condition that a divine Person has taken. It is a marvellous thing that He has taken that condition and died, so that the blood is spoken of as separate from His flesh. It is "drink indeed".

J. H. B. That helps. You have referred to the way in which the assembly is spoken of in the first four chapters of Ephesians, would you say in what way it is regarded in chapter v.?

J. T. It is presented as "subjected to the Christ"; that is the first thing. It is to be noticed that the passage begins the instruction relative to wives, children and bondmen. That is to say, the apostle has in mind that the enemy would take advantage of persons in a subjected condition. In the position of subjection there is great liability to irritation and a consequent giving place to the devil, so that the principle of subjection is introduced in regard of the wives, and then he immediately says, "but even as the assembly is subjected to the Christ, so also wives to their own husbands in everything". That is the first thing. Then you have the love of Christ as the incentive for it: "as the Christ also loved the assembly, and has delivered himself up for it".

F. S. M. Would the deep sleep of Adam suggest to us the impression of the love of Christ, that aspect of His death which was the deep expression of His love?

J. T. The type fails as to love. *God* caused the sleep. Notice it was a *deep* sleep; it was not an ordinary sleep. But you can understand how Eve would speak later of what Adam entered into in order that she might exist. No doubt they had much communion on that point. The Lord would impress us with that too, of where He has been in order that we might have an existence. The very existence of the church depended on it. But here, the moral side is added to that: "in order that he might sanctify it, purifying it by the washing of water by the word". So that the Lord is seen as dealing with us in this tender way; it is "washing of water by the word". "The word" carries with it something very sweet if we consider the relation that exists between the One who is speaking and the one who is being washed. It seems as if it ought to call forth active affections. And the Lord would remind us that the water was due to His death as well. He was actually dead when it flowed.

QUES. And is it not the same kind of love with which the Lord serves the church now, as expressed in the gift of Himself?

J. T. That is right. You cannot get anything more expressive of the love of Christ than this passage. He "loved the assembly, and has delivered himself up for it, in order that he might sanctify it, purifying it by the washing of water by the word, that *he* might present the assembly to himself glorious, having no spot, or wrinkle, or any of such things; but that it might be holy and blameless". The effect of this service is to touch our hearts with the love of Christ, so that our affections are active while in the process. It is no irksome process; it is by the word, but it conveys that He delivered Himself up, that He was actually dead, and that He would have the church in full keeping with eternal thoughts, "without spot or wrinkle or any of such things". It is the ability He has of clearing her of all the effects of sin, so that she answers to Eve before sin came in.

E. S. H. Would "holy and blameless" link on with the opening verses of chapter i.?

J. T. I was just thinking of that: "that we should be holy and blameless before him in love".

REM. So in the Eve type you have the thought of "from eternity to eternity", and all the service of Christ in love that she might be made suitable for eternity.

J. T. That is so; she is taken out of the scene in which moral things have been wrought out, so that she answers to Christ. Hence, while the purpose of God implied the life out of death seen in the church, it also anticipated the moral question that she should go through that, and that gives a certain lustre to her, for the question of holiness arose, not in innocency, but as a consequence of sin.

F. H. B. When he speaks of the washing and the cleansing, I wondered whether he was not looking at the assembly as composed

I

of individuals, and whether that was not the reason he brought in the idea of washing?

J. T. She needs it as formed of those who severally have had part in sin.

F. H. B. But Eve did not need any washing.

J. T. We are not limited to the type here. The Spirit of God does not confine us to Eve in innocency. The church having had to do with the moral question, it has acquired a lustre that answers to Christ, because *He* has had to enter into the moral question, and we should hardly correspond with Him if *we* did not. Eve does not typify holiness, whereas it appears in the church, as, of course, it does in Christ.

C. A. C. There would be an absence of reality if we were to enter into the purpose of God without a reference to the moral side.

J. T. Surely! That is right.

W. R. P. But why should it be necessary for the Lord to go into death if in this aspect of His death it was not the moral side?

J. T. If God intended to have a life seen in the assembly altogether apart from sin and death as its penal consequence, He could surely bring in that figure to indicate it. He intends to have the church in the coming eternity altogether free of any sinful connection, and I think the figure in Genesis ii. is to show that, and to represent God's mind. Not that He had ever such a thought as that Christ should die, save vicariously, but if He had a thought of having the church in a life altogether apart from sin, He is entitled to use a figure to show what was in His mind; and there is ability with Christ to bring the church into a condition and status, in which there is no sense of a past sinful shameful condition. It is "from eternity to eternity", as I was saying, but if it has come down here into the region where moral questions have arisen, this brings it into accord with Christ, because He also came down into that region,—but the primary thought of God is never lost sight of, and that is presented in Genesis ii. It speaks of a life out of death; that is what God intended, but not death as penalty, though it was that as a matter of history, and God foreknew the necessity for this, but if He has in His mind to have something entirely clear of that, He can bring in a type setting that forth. God alone could work out the two things together and maintain them as distinct.

Ques. Then is the love of Christ set forth in that aspect?

J. T. We have just been saying that. It is in the passage here; He "loved the assembly, and has delivered himself up for it".

REM. That is the Adam aspect.

J. T. I think it runs beyond it. The moral question is added to it, in order that Christ might take the church out of the effect of sin and present her to Himself altogether according to Himself, without spot or wrinkle or any such thing. She is wholly free as the bride in the beginning of Revelation xxi. She is adorned for her Husband.

QUES. Is that the view of the love of Christ we should have in the supper?

J. T. Yes, I think it is.

J. H. T. What bearing has "his wife has made herself ready" on this? Does that suppose she has understood the moral question?

J. T. I think so. She is the Lamb's wife, which would mean that she is in accord with the suffering Christ, and it gives lustre to her. Do you not think it is the Colossian side? "I fill up that which is behind of the tribulations of Christ in my flesh, for his body, which is the assembly" (Col. i. 24). She has to go through sufferings, for we would not miss anything of these things in their result. It is the result we have in view.

J. H. T. I should like help as to the "word" as you spoke of it. Is the service of Christ through the gifts in relation to that?

J. T. I think so. He acts mediately now,

but I think we should notice the "washing of water by the word". It is a suggestion of intelligence, and He makes us know what He does. "What I do thou dost not know now, but thou shalt know hereafter" (John xiii. 7). He intends you to know what He does, and that gives great place to the assembly, that what is being done is understood. It is not arbitrary. No husband would act arbitrarily with his wife unless will were in action. The "word" is to convey intelligence, that what is being done is understood, and that greatly helps in ministry.

C. O. B. Do you connect this with John xiii.?

J. T. Yes. The Lord would convey to Peter and to them all, the meaning of what He did. "Unless I wash thee, thou hast not part with me".

M. W. B. The word is the expression of the mind.

H. W. S. Do you connect the thought of subjection with the moral side, or would that go on into eternity?

J. T. The idea of subjection must go on into eternity, even in Christ; "then the Son", it says, "also himself shall be placed in subjection". Eve in innocency was under Adam; he was her head.

A. S. L.   Do you think the deep sleep and the waking out of it would foreshadow in any way what was in the mind and intention of God that it was to be Man of a new order, not the man that came out of dust, but another kind of man altogether was to be the One in whom all His purposes were to centre?

J. T.   That is right, and so John xx. brings before us the "last Adam", and the church, in its members, is seen there also.

W. J. H.   The moral side in Mary Magdalene had already been solved.

J. T.   Yes; out of her had *gone* seven demons.

G. W. W.   I would like to get more clearly what is meant by the "washing of water by the word". Is it the bringing home to the soul morally, of what was set forth and is true in Christ?

J. T.   It is what is set forth in His death—not the blood, but the water. But it is connected with the "word" here. So that we understand the process.

G. W. W.   The bringing us to it, is what is involved in the "washing of water by the word". That is what our brother had in mind when he said that otherwise we should have unreality.

J. T. We should; and therefore we should not be too hasty as "in assembly" to go on to the purpose of God as a matter of light. I think we acquire lustre and power and tone as intelligently bringing in the moral side. But on the other hand, one observes that the brethren often remain too long, in occupation with Christ as Lord; that is, after the supper is eaten, they remain too long before headship and companionship are reached. When we are alongside of Him all the references are to the Father.

G. W. W. Does not that indicate the necessity for ministry on that line? If souls are not really up to the thought of companionship, is not that a special indication for ministry?

J. T. That is what ministry is for: "for the work of the ministry until we all arrive", etc. I believe the Lord uses ministry to enlighten the minds of brethren, but if you get light, the thing is to act on it. As apprehending Christ as Head it is wonderful to be alongside of Him so as to be led of Him to the Father.

Ques. Would that mean that there is intelligent love that enables the saints to be in His presence?

J. T. Yes. When you are with Christ in companionship, there is no thought of any past sinful history, but you must reach that point in the power of the Spirit.

G. W. W. You cannot bring in the question of moral state there.

J. T. You are past it. The Lord's supper implies what is moral; but at such a time as we have referred to we are past that, so that, as scriptures says, "both he that sanctifies and those sanctified are all of one; for which cause he is not ashamed to call them brethren" (Heb. ii. 11). I think if we were occupied unduly with the moral or responsible side, there would be a sense of shame, and you would hardly be equal to the thought of companionship.

M. W. B. You said the moral side was involved in the supper; do you see the combination of the two sides there?

J. T. I think so, but I do not know that we should bring in the penalty. It is more the principle of the *boiling* of the sacrifice, the *in*direct action of judgment. It is that aspect.

M. W. B. That is what I wanted you to make clear. It is not death as penalty in the supper, but rather the expression of love. Would you distinguish between the two?

J. T. The Lord's supper conveys that He gave Himself, and of course we do not wish to shut out what that meant, but both Luke and John leave out the forsaking, and we are entitled to do so under certain circumstances.

J. J. Is that not what the Lord meant in John xv. 13: "Greater love hath no man than this, that a man lay down his life for his *friends*". There was nothing of penalty in that.

J. T. No indeed; you could not in ordinary circumstances, get anything more expressive of love than to lay down one's life, and that is all you need at the supper. Not that you wish to shut out penalty, but if Luke and John leave it out, we can; we need to be occupied more with the *love* side. Matthew and Mark would impress us with the *evidence* of love, but this is not necessary if we are *enjoying it*.

J. H. B. Referring again to Genesis ii., what are we to understand by the words in verse 18: "It is not good that man should be alone; I will make him a helpmate, his like"?

J. T. The words "*Ish*" and "*Ishshah*" indicate correspondence between the two, correspondence in mind and in affection and intelligence.

J. H. B. Would that lead on to the thought of standing before God the Father in association with Him?

J. T. Yes, there is correspondence, as in John xx.

G. W. W. Would you say a little more about the boiling and the roasting?

J. T. I think boiling is to convey to us the indirect action of the fire; the heat reaches the oblation indirectly. If a thing is cooked in a pan the same is true, only that it is more direct than boiling. Boiling is in water; it is to reduce the evidence of the fire. You do not want to leave it out, but to reduce the thought, and I think Luke and John have that in mind. Death is there, of course, as the evidence of love. But Matthew and Mark do not reduce; they give the full bearing of the judgment—the forsaking.

G. W. W. You have the fire direct.

F. H. B. The penalty is more connected with the passover.

J. T. It was "roast with fire". You find complaint sometimes because brethren do not emphasise the forsaking at the Lord's supper, as if it were leaving out something that should be there, but they ought also to complain of Luke and John. If Luke and John did that, we may do it on the same principle.

A. E. M. Would boiling bring in the idea of apprehending the moral question because of what God is?

J. T. You can never leave that out while we are in our present condition, and Luke and John do not leave it out. It is there, but they do not formally mention the forsaking, and I think this helps as to the Lord's supper.

T. R. It is noticeable in Luke that whilst the penalty, the forsaking, is not found there, we have the Spirit of God bringing in the three hours of darkness.

J. T. There is no question in any of the gospels that the judgment of God entered into the death of Christ. We are speaking of how the truth is presented.

A. S. L. In John's epistle propitiation is spoken of as the perfect expression of love: "Herein is love, not that we loved God, but that he loved us, and sent his Son a propitiation for our sins".

J. T. Like Matthew and Mark, that is full testimony, but as in the *enjoyment* of the love we need not bring that side forward.

A. S. L. So that we do not want to be occupied with our sins or past history; we rest in perfect love seen in propitiation.

J. T. Love is thus known and all fear is cast out. Matthew and Mark are the framework of Christianity, meeting the moral question, but not meeting the love question, as formally dealing with it. Luke and John deal more with this, which is important. Luke and John are founded on Matthew and Mark, but they are really the fulness of love. In them you get the Lord coming into the midst of His own after He rose and showing the tokens of His love, but it is not so in Matthew and Mark.

G. W. W. Would you say a word as to the difference between the passover as first partaken of in Exodus xii. and as partaken of in Luke in the upper room?

J. T. In Luke you have much more than you could have in Exodus. You have the judgment expressed in Exodus and the shelter of the blood. They ate the lamb roast with fire in view of the exit from Egypt. The passover that the Lord partook of included additions which He accepted. You find two cups; there is nothing said about them in Exodus. And you find a hymn; there is nothing said about that in Exodus. There was no suggestion of singing in Exodus until chapter xv. It is said that a certain selection of the Psalms were sung at the passover. All this would be of the nature of wealth added, and which the Lord recognized.

G. W. W. So when we take up the expression, "For also our passover, Christ, has been sacrificed", we have to take it up from the standpoint of all that accumulated wealth, and from Luke's standpoint, not from the standpoint of Exodus xii.

J. T. There was something there in connection with which He could link Himself on with them. There were additional elements that He could employ to convey Himself, not in what He was to Israel, but in what He is to the church. There was a certain richness in that passover which does not appear in Exodus.

Eu. R. Do we need in that way to seek to get accumulated wealth in relation to the supper?

J. T. I think so. Whatever wealth there is we should see that in our localities we are not behind. It is a poor thing for the brethren to come and sit down in an impoverished state, with the spiritual elements wanting, that the Lord would use to enhance Himself.

D. L. H. With regard to the cup, I notice that it says as regards the passover, that He took *a* cup, but when the cup is referred to in the Lord's supper, He took *the* cup. I apprehend that means that He took the cup which had already been used in the passover and gave it a further application in the supper.

J. T. At that time there were several cups

used according to historical accounts, so that the article being affixed to the cup of the Lord's supper makes it all the more important. There was a vessel there for His use, and practically as coming together we must see that there is nothing absent that the Lord might use.

QUES. Would you say a little more about being by the side of Christ in view of the Father?

J. T. That all enters into this. As headship is apprehended, the idea of the assembly comes into evidence. The apostle goes on here to refer to Eve again. "For no one has ever hated his own flesh, but nourishes and cherishes it, even as also the Christ the assembly: for we are members of his body; we are of his flesh, and of his bones. Because of this a man shall leave his father and mother, and shall be united to his wife, and the two shall be one flesh. This mystery is great, but I speak as to Christ, and as to the assembly". As we come into the sense of companionship with Christ, we understand that He is not ashamed to call us brethren; we come to the idea of the church as of Him. Then there is no sense of previous sinful history. That is a point to be reached as we come together in assembly.

QUES. Would Mary Magdalene standing by the side of Christ immediately He came out of death be a nucleus of the church?

J. T. I think so. She calls Him, "Rabboni", meaning that she needs instruction. That is essential here. Rabboni is "my teacher", and presently He says to her, "Touch me not, for I have not yet ascended to my Father; but go to my brethren and say to them, I ascend to my Father and your Father, and to my God and your God. Mary of Magdala comes bringing word to the disciples that she had seen the Lord, and that he had said these things to her". I think there you have, in principle, the church. She is in subjection to Christ as taught. She does not assume the place of a teacher with the disciples, but simply tells them that He had said these things to her. There is no idea of authority with her, but simply that she is the bearer of a message. The Lord comes and He says, "Peace", and shows them His hands and His side. There is a clear indication that they were the objects of His love, and that, so to speak, they had come out of His side; and then He breathes on them.

H. H. Does not that indicate that the saints should be viewed as risen as the Lord comes into the midst?

J. T. The platform is ascension. "I ascend" is not historical there, but characteristic, so that He enters in that light. The church is really the product of an ascended Christ. It comes out of death with Him, as of Him, taking its character from Him as risen and ascended.

H. H. I was thinking of the first part of the meeting for the supper, which allows for the wilderness side of things, and in that connection you do not exactly regard the saints as risen, but to join Christ in companionship you do have to appreciate them as risen, that is, Christ comes into the midst as One who is risen.

J. T. You must add the thought of ascension. That is important because it gives the church its place as we have it in Ephesians. I think Matthew, Mark and Luke, have in view the church as in the wilderness; the Lord's supper is in the wilderness. The position answers to the type of Zipporah, I think; it is a question of what she makes herself to be. In Exodus she is brought to Moses after deliverance is effected at mount Horeb, and her two sons are referred to there. There is only one son mentioned in chapter ii. whose name meant that Moses was a "stranger in a strange land"; but the second son's name means, "God . . . has delivered me from the sword of Pharaoh"; that is, deliverance, realized in the wilderness. But in Numbers, the official class represented in Aaron and Miriam, complain against Moses because he had married an Ethiopian woman. That is what comes out in the wilderness. It shows the responsibility that attaches to the church in the wilderness, and what opposition may arise in these circumstances. But while beginning thus in the wilderness, in the assembly, we go on to Canaan.

Eu. R. Did I understand you to say the church is derived from an *ascended* Christ?

J. T. Quite so; it is heavenly. It comes out of heaven and goes back to heaven. There is no thought of Zipporah going into the land; Achsah is that side; she wants the inheritance, and she wants it in the most favourable relations. She had a south land, but she wanted springs of water to maintain her in the full height of her blessing. Coming back to Moses and the wilderness, it says in Canticles, "Who is this that cometh up from the wilderness, leaning upon her beloved?" (chap. viii. 5). We may think little of the church in the wilderness, but the Lord will bring her through. Who is she? She is leaning upon Him; she is dependent upon Him, and

K

she is not out of keeping with Him either. He brings us through, and therefore it is a serious matter to be complaining because of the unloveliness of the brethren, as Aaron and Miriam did with regard to the Ethiopian woman. Of course it is a humbling thing if they are unlovely, but the complaint is against Christ. He has taken us on, and He will bring us up out of the wilderness.

N. McC. Would coming up out of the wilderness bring us to the point of companionship?

J. T. Well, it is not quite so far. She is *leaning* on Him. It is not exactly companionship; it is in the land that we join Him as His companions, and the ground is thus completely changed.

F. H. B. I think our weakness is in the lack of the consciousness of companionship with Christ. We speak a good bit about Him and to Him, but we have not the *sense* of companionship. As you said, if we had we would speak to the Father.

J. T. And we should be conscious thus of being equal with Him. Not of course having part in His Deity, but "he that sanctifies and those sanctified are all of one; for which cause he is not ashamed to call them brethren". They come up with Him out of death, and there is no other history. He has been down, and they have come up with Him, and I think that is where we touch what we have here, that we are "of his flesh and of his bones". It speaks in the Psalm of our being curiously wrought in the lower parts of the earth.

J. H. B. What is meant by the expression "union with Christ"?

J. T. It means that I am *of Him* and so united to Him. "The two shall be one flesh". It is mysterious; I doubt whether it could be defined in words.

J. H. B. It is a little different from the thought of companionship.

J. T. It goes beyond companionship. "The two shall be one"; it is a remarkable thought.

J. J. Is union greater than unity? I thought the Lord would not unite with Himself what is not united here. We are united together and then union follows.

C. O. B. Is the presentation of verse 27 future?

J. T. "That he might present the assembly to himself, glorious, having no spot, or wrinkle, or any of such things". I think it would enter into our relations in the assembly now; but properly, it is future. It is the Lord looking on to the presentation of the whole church to Himself.

"This mystery is great, but I speak as to Christ, and as to the assembly." We are left with that here, the almost inscrutable thought of Christ and the church. You are cast on the Lord and the Spirit to understand it. It is really more for understanding than for definition; it is called a mystery, but he says, "I speak as to Christ, and as to the assembly". That is what the Holy Spirit would leave with us.

VI

READING

EPHESIANS VI. 10–24

J. T. The subject this afternoon is the conflict. It seems fitting that this subject should
be found at the close of this epistle, for whilst
opening up to us the counsels of God culminating in the coming eternity, the epistle
contemplates us as here, where the enemy's
power is. That is, if God would entrust all
this precious knowledge to us, we should
contend for and stand in it. As we have
noted already as to the subjects in our several
readings, the types serve well in unfolding
this subject to us. Whilst the Old Testament
is but little alluded to in the epistle, yet it
stresses spirituality, and spirituality will avail
itself of all that there is in the way of spiritual
help and furnishings. So that the subject
requires for the right understanding of it in
detail references to the Old Testament, particularly to Joshua as the typical military
man, and to David too. Joshua is not only
a type of Christ as the Leader of His people

militarily, but a type for young believers as to how they come into the conflict and learn to fight. That is, after the gift of the Spirit according to Exodus xvii., the enemy attacks at once, so that the idea of spiritual warfare is seen in that chapter. The Amalekites attack and you have the initial idea of spiritual warfare, the leader in the conflict, Joshua, being still young. It may be advantageous that we should begin with this part of the subject, so that the young brothers present may follow, and see that the idea of military service and conflict begins at once, as they receive the Spirit of God.

H. D'A. C. Military service begins at once.

J. T. Yes, as we receive the Spirit according to Exodus xvii. Then in Numbers we are marshalled in relation to the standard of our fathers' houses, having something definitely to protect. But in Exodus xvii. the young believer is pictured as coming into the conflict with Amalek. For Christians this is individual and inward.

D. L. H. In connection with the conflict with Amalek, was not the effort of the enemy to keep the people immediately from the purpose of God?

J. T. That would be the thought, the Holy Spirit being given as the earnest of the inheritance.

A. S. L. Does Amalek represent Satan?

J. T. Satan working in the flesh especially in young believers. Spiritual conflict begins there. Joshua is the spiritual leader. Moses says, "Choose *us* men". The conflict is not to be on party lines in any way; it is in relation to *all*.

A. S. L. And success depended on intercession.

J. T. It is a hidden matter, and there is a measure of uncertainty about it. Victory is not immediately granted, because we are to *learn* war. When victory is not immediately granted we become dependent. We have a wily foe. There was a swaying and uncertainty, all hinging on Moses' upheld arms. That would not allude to any weakness in Christ now as interceding for us, but weakness in our reliance on Him.

A. S. L. In our chapter our conflict is "not against blood and flesh, but against principalities, against authorities, against the universal lords of this darkness, against spiritual power of wickedness in the heavenlies". It is satanic power.

J. T. It is not Satan in the flesh here; it is spiritual wickedness in *heavenly* places, but in order to have part in this great universal conflict in the heavenlies, young brothers have to learn war, to meet Satan himself in contending for the truth. We must understand how to deal with spiritual opposition. Joshua in Exodus xvii. represents the spiritual leader, that is to say, Christ known in that small way first. In learning war we grow in the apprehension of the intercession on high, and of the Lord as our spiritual Leader in the conflict.

E. S. H. So that you know where to turn. It says of Joshua that he "broke the power of Amalek".

E. J. H. It is not the believer that takes the initiative with Amalek. As soon as the believer has the Spirit, the enemy attacks.

J. T. He forces it on you, and that is of God.

E. J. H. So it is intended that every young believer should be a man of war.

J. T. The great progenitor of faith had "trained servants" in his house,—that is the idea, and he used them to rescue his brother. They were trained, and there were three hundred and eighteen of them. I think the training for war begins in Exodus, and then in Numbers, we are marshalled and set up locally, in relation to the testimony. Now we have something to defend.

J. H. T. Do you get the idea in Paul in Acts xiii. 9? He was filled with the Holy

Spirit in meeting one whom he calls "son of the devil". John Mark goes back at that point.

J. T. Mark was unequal to the conflict then.

A. S. L. This conflict is not exactly reserved for those far advanced in the faith.

J. T. No; and so I thought it would be advantageous to the young, to see that we are brought into it at once. It is forced upon us, and God uses it, that we might learn war, for He has a great deal for us to defend and protect, as the sequel showed in the books of Numbers and Joshua. Numbers is rather a defensive warfare, but Joshua is attack. It is to take the inheritance and stand in it; but Numbers is to protect what is set up in the tabernacle.

A. S. L. So it would be young believers who have been granted some apprehension of their place in the church.

J. T. Yes. I think Exodus xvii. is very much like Romans; but Numbers is more Corinthians, what there is in a collective sense to be defended in the wilderness.

Eu. R. And does not Joshua accept a kind of training under Moses?

J. T. He does. As a young man he was lacking in a good ear for *sounds*. Coming down from the mountain in Exodus xxxii. with Moses, he thought it was the sound of war, but he was mistaken. Military operations require a good ear and good eyesight.

QUES. Was the apostle teaching Timothy war in the second epistle?

J. T. He was calling upon him to be a "good soldier of Jesus Christ".

A. S. L. Is there a difference between Joshua and Ephesians in respect of conflict, that in Ephesians we are exhorted to stand as being there, whereas Joshua, as you said, had to be aggressive, to go forward and attack?

J. T. We have to be aggressive, but I suppose this epistle contemplates the land as already taken; the territory was all taken by apostolic service, and it is for the saints to hold the ground.

M. W. B. There was warfare in connection with Sihon and Og. What is the difference between that kind of conflict and the conflict in Joshua?

J. T. That is still wilderness conflict. I think that Sihon and Og have allusion to the territory that Moses gives us. It is a question of the authority of the Lord. There is territory given to us on the principle of

authority, that is by Moses; and then there
is territory given to us by Joshua which is
rather spiritual leadership. Rahab spoke of
what the people did to Sihon and Og. She
knew what Jehovah did at the Red Sea, and
what the people did to Sihon and Og. I
think it alludes to the believer as himself
belonging to God, that God has rights in
him. It is what occurs in the believer after
he *recognizes* the Spirit. It is the overthrow
of the "big I"; that is one of the greatest
struggles. That is not in Exodus xvii.; which
is rather the way I am troubled by Satan
interfering and working through the flesh
before I understand Romans vii. But the
victory over Sihon and Og, is after the Holy
Spirit is formally recognized. That is to say,
it is Romans viii., and the great battle then
is whether it is to be Christ in me, in His
rights over me, or whether it is to be the "big
I", that is to say, the big man, Og. His overthrow is a great victory.

M. W. B. It is all in relation to the wilderness, and to self in some form. But the warfare in 2 Corinthians x.—"the overthrow of
strongholds; overthrowing reasonings and
every high thing that lifts itself up against
the knowledge of God"—does that go further
or is it still some element of the "big I"?

J. T. That goes beyond the battle with Og. Paul speaks of the weapons of *his* warfare; they were not carnal. They had not even overcome the "big I" at Corinth; that was the difficulty with the leaders.

M. W. B. Then the question of self coming into the wilderness sphere, shows that that question might arise even after taking up a military position in respect of the testimony in Numbers.

J. T. Yes, quite so.

M. W. B. Do you think that affords the testing circumstances for the exposure of this "I"?

J. T. I think it does. You get a brother who attends the meetings, he is so far set for the testimony, but in how many of us is self overthrown? One can speak feelingly, because the fact that I am in fellowship and contend for the truth and the principles of the house of God does not prove, in itself, that I have overcome Sihon and Og, because it is a question of the rights of the Lord in *me*. He would be in me instead of myself. "If Christ be in you, the body is dead"; that is the overthrow of Og.

A. S. L. That comes after the brazen serpent.

J. T. It does; the overthrow of Sihon and Og is after that.

E. J. H. Do you get that in spirit in Matthew xviii. where you humble yourself to come into the kingdom?

J. T. Exactly. You can see how self stood out even after all the light of the mount of transfiguration. They were talking of who was to be greatest in the kingdom of the heavens. So the Lord called a little child to Him and set him down and said, "Unless ye are converted and become as little children, ye will not at all enter into the kingdom of the heavens".

W. C. How does Phinehas come in here? Numbers xxv.?

J. T. That would be priestly zeal, as Paul came in at Corinth.

The issue at Corinth was Midianitish. It belongs to the conflict in Numbers. It is a question of worldly associations.

Phinehas was later sent out against the Midianites with twelve thousand of Israel. It was a continuation of the principle of warfare in Phinehas; it is priestly. You are concerned about the holiness of the people of God, that they should be saved from worldly associations. To Phinehas the priesthood was established for ever.

QUES. Does the expression here, "Be strong in the Lord", suggest that self has been

abandoned for Christ, and you have taken
up a new position?

J. T. I think so. The Lord is now domin-
ant; but in this chapter it is not the Lord,
as in Romans. It is not a question of the
kingdom, but a military title; He is Lord
militarily. It corresponds with Acts xix. In
chapter xviii. where we have the wilderness
in view, that is, Corinth, it is God—"the
word of *God*"—but in Acts xix. where the
land is in view, it is the Lord—"the word
of the *Lord*". The latter is what is in view
in this passage: "be strong in the Lord, and
in the might of his strength".

F. H. B. Does Joshua represent the Lord
Himself or the Spirit of Christ in the
saints?

J. T. He is Christ apprehended in a spiritual, military way. Joshua is the spiritual
leader as we have seen, introduced in scripture in a military way. His ministry corresponds with Ephesians, whereas the ministry
or leadership of Moses enters into Romans
and Corinthians. That is, it is a question of
Christ's authority over the saints, whereas
Joshua is a question of spiritual power and
leadership in warfare, placing us in Canaan.

QUES. Where does Caleb come in on that
line?

J. T. Caleb represents the faith and energy in the believer that takes possession of the inheritance. He valued his own portion, Hebron, a portion divinely given to him, and he dislodged the enemy there. In Caleb we see sustained military ability to an advanced age.

QUES. What about Othniel?

J. T. Othniel would be Christ obtaining the church through warfare.

EU. R. Where does the "captain of the Lord's host" come in?

J. T. He refers to this epistle. The great military service in Joshua begins as the people are set up at Gilgal. The conflict begins at Jericho. Here a man stands over against Joshua with a drawn sword in his hand. Now this is for Joshua's education; he is to be on new ground in the warfare; he is to understand it is not partisan, but a question of *Jehovah's* host, so that when Joshua says, "Art thou for us, or for our enemies?" the man says, "No; for as captain of the army of Jehovah am I now come". The position in Joshua therefore, is that there is a captain of Jehovah's host, and He is no less than a divine Person, because Joshua was to take his shoes off his feet before Him. Holiness was to enter into the warfare; selfish thoughts were to be excluded.

F. H. B. Is the object of the warfare here to maintain the full testimony of the Christ, and not simply to secure our inheritance? The Man with the drawn sword said He was captain of the army of Jehovah.

J. T. Exactly; so in the next chapter in Joshua the *ark* is prominent. Having the captain, you have also the power in which the conflict is carried on. So that the ark, accompanied by the blowing of the trumpets, is carried round the city, and on the seventh day it encircles the city seven times, when the shout brings the wall down. We are taught in all this that "the excellency of the power is of God"; that is, we have no strength at all in ourselves. In the ark and trumpets, there is a definite presentation of the testimony in Christ brought into view. The Lord said, "I have overcome the world", not only Satan, but the world, and I think the apostles in their testimony overcame the world. In principle it is overcome for us.

J. J. Would the four gospels help us in connection with putting on the whole armour of God? You see the Lord invulnerable there.

J. T. Yes. The armour of God is seen there. The Lord overcame by the manifestation of the features we have here. We do well to weigh the facts at Jericho because they

put us into our place; the power is of God.
It is in the clear sounding out of the testimony
and the presentation of Him who is the
subject of it, that the world is thus brought
down. But in the bringing down of the world
you look after those that are to be saved.
Rahab represents them.

H. H.   Do you mean the world as a system?

J. T.   Yes, and the things by which it is
kept going, such as the books and the seven
sons of Sceva, that is, the perfection of spiritual
wickedness in persons who have apostatised
from God.

H. H.   We have, of course, to judge all
that for ourselves; much has thus to follow
in our souls' history after we receive the
gospel.

QUES.   Does the apprehension of the truth
of the Son of God help us in overcoming the
world?

J. T.   Scripture says so. "This is the victory
which has gotten the victory over the world,
our faith. Who is he that gets the victory
over the world, but he that believes that
Jesus is the Son of God" (1 John v. 4, 5). I
apprehend that this epistle is specially included in "our faith", which faith has overcome the world. It involves another system,
and moral superiority over the present one;

L

so that, although I move about in it, the world has no influence over me. That seen in a number of Christians shows what God has effected—there is something set up here that has overcome the world, "our faith".

W. J. H. Do you think that "Jesus is the Son of God" would be a conception of the ark, so small outwardly, yet infinitely great and powerful? I was thinking of what the demons said in regard of the sons of Sceva: "Jesus I know". Jesus is His name in the lowly conditions He took and yet He is powerful enough for them to know Him.

J. T. "Who is he that gets the victory over the world, but he that believes that *Jesus* is the Son of God"—that lowly One, all power being in Him.

QUES. Would that be illustrated in the way they brought their books and burned them at Ephesus?

J.T. Exactly. Othniel took that city, the "city of the books"; that was a particular feature that Caleb had in his mind to be overcome. It is a formidable element of the world—"the power of the press", as men say. Very few of the people of God are free of damaging literature. It is sometimes said that there is so much ministry printed that brethren have not time to read it, but one large daily newspaper contains more reading matter than one of our books.

S. J. B. C. I suppose Kirjath-arba would be the city of human power; and Kirjath-sepher would be the *wisdom* of the world.

J. T. Yes. Kirjath-sepher would be the Greek world, and Kirjath-arba the Roman, the world of power. I refer to the period when the world was overthrown by the testimony of the apostles.

QUES. Would you mind saying a little more about the Man with the drawn sword in His hand? One feels a little difficulty as to the distinction between him and Joshua.

J. T. I think Joshua, there, represents any one of us as in the warfare. Warfare tends to taking sides by those engaged in it. I have something in my mind that I would like to attain and I crave for some one to help me. What happened at Jericho, is to remind us that the Lord will have no part in that at all. I get no help from Him in that relation. Joshua asks, "Art thou for us or for our enemies?" The first time Joshua is told to take the sword to lead in a battle, Moses says, "Choose *us* men", meaning for *all* the people of God, not for any section of them. I do not believe Joshua was free from partisan bias in his early life; in Numbers we are told that when God would extend the Spirit by bringing a greater personnel into the ministry than one man, and Eldad and Medad were actually prophesying, Joshua said, "My lord Moses, forbid them". He did not wish anybody to prophesy but Moses. Apparently he was not clear of partisan tendencies, even at Jericho. He enquires, "Art thou for us, or for our enemies"? The Man with the drawn sword answers, "No; for as captain of the army of Jehovah am I now come".

E. J. H. Does Peter come to that when he says, "our beloved brother Paul"?

J. T. Yes. After the incident at Antioch, where evidently partisan spirit existed, it is very beautiful that he could refer to Paul in that way.

J. J. Would you bring David into this chapter as well as Joshua—he took the stronghold of Zion? He moved on from Hebron to do that. Would the Jebusite (2 Sam. v.) refer to spiritual wickednesses?

J. T. Yes. Joshua places us in the inheritance, but, after we are there we find enemies. Some were allowed to stay in the land. David's work involved subjugation of internal and external enemies. David's service was imperial; he was king of kings and lord of lords. He foreshadowed Christ as seen in Revelation xix.

C. C. E. Is there any distinction spiritually between Jericho and the rest of the seven nations?

J. T. Jericho is representative of all, I think, it represents the power of the world. Israel were faced with it immediately, so that the coming down of its walls, as they did without Israel having to strike a blow, would mean that the power in the conflict was of God and not of men. I think it was, in principle, the whole entrenched power of the enemy. It typifies what is before us here— "The universal lords of this darkness . . . spiritual power of wickedness in the heavenlies". Jericho was evidently very well fortified.

Ques. Were not the seven kings in Jericho? Would not Joshua xxiv. 11 indicate that?

J. T. I do not think it means that they were actually in Jericho, but rather that Jericho represented, as we were saying, the whole territory of the seven kings in the land of Canaan. The conquest of the land is in view there, as the context shows.

F. H. B. What would be the difference between the overthrow of Jericho and the five kings that he destroyed afterwards?

J. T. The curse came on them; the captains put their feet on the necks of those kings and then they were hanged. In the book of

Joshua all the conquered kings were enu-
merated. Hazor was "the head of all those
kingdoms", it is said. Rome was in the same
position at the time of the apostles. Hazor
was burnt with fire. Instead of Rome being
constituted the head of Christendom, the type
would teach us that it was overcome. Nothing
that marked the world's city was to be incor-
porated in the city of God, the church answering to this. The whole system of Romanism
is developed out of Rome the head of the
nations, the empire taking on a spiritual garb;
and I suppose the burning of Hazor would
mean that that which it represents must be
utterly repudiated by the people of God.

J. H. T. It says, "they left none that
breathed" (Joshua xi. 14). It is a striking
expression.

J. T. It is. Hazor later recovered strength,
as we learn in the book of Judges, with remarkable rapidity; we read also of Jabin its king
and Sisera the captain of his host living in
another place (chap. iv. 2). There was great
confidence between them and mutual reliance;
that was the power Deborah had to deal with.
He was "king of Canaan" answering, I think,
to what Romanism has become. But Deborah
says to Barak, "Hath not Jehovah the God
of Israel commanded? Go and draw towards

mount Tabor". This indicates the way we overcome that kind of evil; it is by recognizing the commandment of the Lord. "Hath not Jehovah the God of Israel commanded?" Deborah says. She was a remarkable woman in a military sense, and her song with Barak shows the great military energy that filled her soul. She was dealing with an intrepid enemy, one in the place of head, which Rome has always arrogated to itself. Sisera was overthrown by obedience to God's commandment: Barak with ten thousand men should draw towards Mount Tabor, meaning that now it is a question of military manœuvres or tactics, so that you have the advantage in the battlefield; a very important matter in warfare. The Lord selected the battlefield, and it is important for young believers to understand that the battle is the Lord's and victory is sure as we are obedient. God says to Barak, "I will draw unto thee, to the torrent Kishon, Sisera, the captain of Jabin's army, and his chariots and his multitude". The army of Sisera had thus a great disadvantage, and the issue in favour of Israel was certain. We are taught in all these incidents what is meant here, how *we* are to be in the conflict, because we have a wily foe operating in a very wide sphere. By and by he will come up "on the breadth of the earth", after the millennium, as we are told in Revelation xx. Satan will have a free hand on the earth, on the whole breadth of it, to encircle the camp of the saints. But fire from heaven consumes his army. Now it is not the earth but the heavenly places, because it is a question of the conflict of the church.

H. H. Is there not a striking allusion to the apprehension of headship in Judges? Are not the facts in the light of the headship of Christ? Outwardly things are in disorder, no king in Israel. Deborah was a woman, but she got Barak to move, and Jael was the *wife* of Heber the Kenite.

J. T. Yes; and it is said of Deborah that she was the *wife* of Lapidoth. They were both in subjection, but Deborah had evidently gained a moral victory over herself. She dwelt under her *own* palm tree. She refers to Jael as preceding her, mentioning her with Shamgar. In their days the highways were unoccupied, that is, the principles of God had not been attended to. So it seems Jael was not on the same spiritual level as Deborah, but she slew Sisera, and Deborah magnificently renders tribute to her.

J. H. B. Does the conflict in Ephesians vi. go on together, or is it what we do individually?

J. T.   I think it is collective. It is universal and I believe involves the "unity of the Spirit" and the "unity of the faith". I do not see how we can meet this combination of darkness unless we hold universally the "unity of the Spirit" and the "unity of the faith". The Lord would have us drop all localism and nationalism, and move together in the light of the assembly and its heavenly places and privileges.

M. W. B.   Is that the link with Psalm lxviii. from which the verse is quoted in Ephesians iv.: "Thou hast ascended on high, thou hast led captivity captive: thou hast received gifts in Man"?

J. T.   I think so. The Lord having gone on high leading captivity captive, the power is in His hands, and His giving gifts to men implies the power of the Spirit specifically expressed. As we were saying the other day, and which I think is worthy of notice, the mighty men come in immediately after David's anointing in 1 Chronicles; but in 2 Samuel they come in at the end. I do not think we should minimise what there is in the last days, for they are in a certain way equal to the first days, and I think the mighties go right through. Samuel would show that they go right through, that no one of that character is omitted from the list. Whatever they were at the beginning, as in Chronicles, they also have their place at the end.

M. W. B. So that links on the days of Acts xix.—the overthrow of the power of evil at Ephesus—with the present time; and our exercises to-day should have the same end in view.

J. T. That is the way to bring this chapter into the present time. The same circumstances exist;—Christ is in heaven and the Holy Spirit is on earth, and the gifts are here; there is the possibility of mighty men to lead on the people of God, and to hold the ground that God has restored to us.

P. L. Are the mighties found at the end in 2 Timothy? "Only Luke is with me"; "take Mark"; "Prisca and Aquila, and the house of Onesiphorus".

J. T. They are mighty surely.

H. H. You get a good list at the end of Romans of church material.

J. T. Yes. The many salutations of Paul would give those mentioned a status in Rome that would greatly assist in leading them into the inheritance. Immediately after the salutations the apostle goes on to speak of the assembly.

J. H. B. Then if in Ephesians the enemies are viewed in the heavenlies, where are the saints viewed as standing?

J. T. In the light of our calling—the church's place. A comparison with Revelation xii. will show that the final conflict is in the heavenlies, Michael leading, to drive out Satan and his army. That would be to make room for the church literally there. Now it is a faith period, so that we are contending on the principle of faith for all these things. The heavenlies belong to the church; we have prior rights there. Satan should not be there; it is a question of holding in faith the heavenly position—and unitedly too.

H. H. Do we not combat with the influence of wicked spirits on the minds of people through bad doctrine. This might get in even amongst the saints?

J. T. Yes surely. That is how the enemy is working. He is operating from a great central spiritual position on the minds of men here; he reaches us in that way. It may reach us in a multitude of ways, but we are to have on, not only the armour of light, as in Romans, but the whole armour of God. Thus the whole position is held.

H. H. We know our place on high.

J. T. And your walk and ways are in keeping with it; you are *standing* in the full light of the calling.

H. H. The armour would protect you there.

J. T. It would.

M. W. B. You referred just now to the "unity of the Spirit" and the "unity of the faith" in special connection with this. Would you say a little how that works out?

J. T. I think that is very important because it is a universal thing here; it is universal and collective. Of course we are in the greatest weakness, but the chapter is light for us as to how we are held together in the over-throw of all that marks the world. The world is being led on to the idea of a head and a central position, which is working out now on the Continent. The most potent opposition is organized opposition, and God meets that by organization. Matthew shows that the Lord met *two* demoniacs, *two* blind men, and so on. It is a question of organization. Chapter iv. of this epistle is divine organization. That is to say, we are bound up in spiritual affections,—which would mean that I cannot afford to lose my brother. And so you have the word to Paul on the ship, Acts xxvii., that God had given to him all that sailed

with him. That ought to be the desire of
every one of us—not to lose one. Well, that
implies the unity of the Spirit; it is a question
of affection. As we saw yesterday, Absalom's
kingdom was thus overthrown in Jerusalem.
For that you have the unity of the Spirit,
but then there is also the unity of the faith,
which would mean the superiority of Christian
truth, the truth that God has restored—the
wonderful unfolding of the mind of God before
which no philosopher could ever stand. The
books were burnt because they were shown
to be falacious. This was because of the great
superiority of the truth. Paul's ministry at
Ephesus involved the most wonderful unfolding of the truth and counsels of God, so he
says, "I have not shrunk from announcing
to you all the counsel of God". Hence the
intelligence the Ephesians had, and that I
think is what is involved in the unity of the
faith; so that you have the unity of the Spirit,
and the unity of the faith, and the self-action
of the body. Instead of being overcome you
have a system of things that is invulnerable.
Walking in the light and practical acceptance
of all this, God gives us the victory in the
conflict.

QUES. "Having accomplished all things, to
stand"? What are the "all things"?

J. T. Whatever was obligatory on them; they were to *stand*; not give up any ground, but hold what was secured for them.

J. H. T. Is there time to say a word about the panoply of God?

J. T. It is the *whole* armour, what has marked God in coming into this world in which Satan was entrenched. How in Christ He met the evil. The gospels show how Christ met all opposition. I think we learn in that way; but these varied parts of the armour are most instructive and practical. "Stand therefore, having girt about your loins with truth"; that is the first thing. Then the breastplate of righteousness, and the preparation of the glad tidings of peace on the feet; and then, besides all this, the shield of faith "with which ye will be able to quench all the inflamed darts of the wicked one". "Have also the helmet of salvation". Those are all armour; and then, the "sword of the Spirit", by which you defend yourself and also go forward in attack.

Eu. R. You referred to the captain of the Lord's host as suggesting a divine Person; do you connect it with the title "Lord" in this chapter, and that it is a divine Person who has the situation in hand?

J. T. That is exactly the truth.

THE SELECTION AND FORMATION
OF SERVANTS

ADDRESS BY J.T.

Acts ix. 15, 16; Matt. iv. 19; John xiii. 23.

I have in mind, dear brethren, to speak about service, and to show, in so doing, how it entered into our dispensation and became diversified there. The best features of everything are seen in this dispensation, and so, whilst service and servants appear throughout the Old Testament, they do not rise to the level of our times. In our dispensation we have the idea presented in perfection in our Lord Jesus Christ, "Who," as we read, "subsisting in the form of God, did not esteem it an object of rapine to be on an equality with God; but emptied himself, taking a bondman's form" (Phil. ii. 6, 7). So that we have One here in whom the idea of service is fully and perfectly presented, according to the prophetic word, "Behold my servant whom I uphold, mine elect in whom my soul delighteth" (Isa. xlii. 1). I commend that word at the outset, for it conveys to us how deeply divine feelings were engaged and moved as Jesus appeared here as a Bondman.

I wish to show from the three servants mentioned in the passages read, the prominent varieties, such as were intended to give character to the dispensation from the beginning to the end, the first representing election, for the Lord in answering Ananias says, referring to Saul, "Go, for this man is an *elect* vessel to me". I wish to dwell on the Lord's word as to this servant before he began to serve, as conveying what I may call the most unique feature of service, namely, that it is the outcome of divine selection. But then to go over the other points briefly, in Simon Peter we have one who was *made* a servant, which is the second point; the Lord saying to him with his brother, "I will make you fishers of men"; the third feature as seen in John, being *lovability*.

I wish to speak to you under those three heads, because they enter importantly into service, and must combine if service is to be effectual; the first corresponding strikingly with Christ Himself, who is formally said to be Jehovah's Elect One, in whom His soul delighted.

Election as to the servant is not the same as election for eternity. The latter refers to all believers. The former is very special and has the testimony in view; but it implies great forethought on the part of the Lord and preparation of the vessel, the word "vessel", in this sense, being peculiar to Paul. It implies that the Lord has gone a long way up the stream, so to speak, and looked after the forefathers, the training and the environment of the person selected. So that the apostle Paul was in the Lord's mind long before He called him. He had elected him, and He had elected him with a view to a certain use, in which only he could be employed, and He had in mind that no one should displace him. In the course of his testimony, he became very much disliked by many, even some whom he had served at the cost of his life. They might not object to his ministry and teaching, but they would in time prefer that some one else should be doing the teaching and the preaching. But the Lord had elected this servant, He had a work for him to do which was special, and He was determined that no one should displace him. So, at the end of his ministry, he says that the Lord stood by him—to deliver him from the lion's mouth, but not only that, but rather that *by him* the preaching might be *fully* known. Some might think that others could preach as well as he, but this was not the

M

Lord's mind; He determined that the preaching should be fully presented in this great vessel that He had elected. No one else could have done it; there was not a man in the whole world that could preach like Paul. I do not say that as a gratuitous statement, but that we might see that his preaching was peculiar to himself, a preaching that the Lord intended to use, so that the thing preached should be fully known. I do not believe that in any address of Paul's there would be anything to detract from the preaching. In fact, so emphatic is he about this that he says, "If our gospel be hid, it is hid to them that are lost" (2 Cor. iv. 3); and he says further, "We preach not ourselves, but Christ Jesus the Lord; and ourselves your servants for Jesus' sake" (2 Cor. iv. 5).

Those first mentioned by the Lord to be served by Paul are the *nations*; then *kings*, and then the *sons of Israel*. He was to bear the Lord's name before nations. The world under the government of God is composed of nations. God intervened according to Genesis xi., early in the history of mankind, after the flood, to separate it into nations, meaning that a centralized combination as at Shinar, would hinder the testimony. Then you find with the nations thus formed, that the Spirit of

God returns to the posterity of Shem, that being the line in which the testimony should come to the nations. It is as if God were to say, "I have created circumstances in My government, which will admit of the nations, in due course, being reached." But each of the nations had its own interests and aspirations, and so it required skill, that the preaching, in the name of the Lord Jesus, might be carried to each of them. Paul used the utmost care in preaching to the nations, so that there should be no prejudice aroused, and yet that he should be able to take out from each of them, a people, detached from its own national traits, so as to be linked on with those taken out of the other nations. It was a wonderful piece of work, and he speaks of it as "the offering up of the nations" (Rom. xv. 16). He was carrying on a kind of sacrificial service, "that the offering up of the nations might be acceptable, sanctified by the Holy Spirit". It was no question with him of numbers; you will not find specific numbers in connection with Paul's converts, whereas you do find numbers specifically mentioned in connection with the preaching of Peter and the others at Pentecost, for numbers have reference to the "treasure" (Matt. xiii. 44). When you come to treasure, then the idea of counting comes in, and this came out at Pentecost. The Lord had secured the field, and He was now asserting His right to take the treasure out of it, and so you find numbers —one hundred and twenty first of all, then three thousand, and so on. But with Paul, it is one idea; it is not a question with him of numbers, although of course there were numbers. What is in mind with him is the pearl, that is, *one* idea. How little we know in service about one idea; but I can see that a man governed by one idea, is sure to be effective. There was with Paul this controlling thought, to secure one thing—the church—for Christ. That involved great care in preaching to the nations, that those taken out of each should be detached from it and linked up as one, with all believers from the other nations. All this is a feature of Paul's ministry.

Then in regard of *kings*, you see how he bore the name of Christ before them. I do not know how one would do in the presence of a king, but I believe that the Lord never intended that the gospel should come in among men by the back door, so to speak. This is very practical, because if we are to bear the Lord's name the idea is not to go to the servants or to the poor *only*; the idea is to go to influential men, and that needs courage. Hence

you find in the types that Moses is directed to
go down by the river in the morning, the
Lord telling him that Pharaoh is going down
there. The morning thus mentioned would
mean that there was much to be done in the
day opening up, and the instruction to Moses
was to "stand . . . in front of him" (Exod.
vii. 15). Now look at that scene! There is a
man classified as a Hebrew, under reproach,
and he is to take up this attitude before the
King. Indeed no one is any good in the service unless he is consciously under reproach.
I should never approach a king on the ground
of my identity in this world, however great it
might be. A man might be called out of great
dignity in this world, and think he could go
and preach to a company like himself, but
that is not the divine thought. The divine
idea is that the preacher is under reproach—
the reproach of Christ. This Hebrew is by
the river with the word in his heart to stand
in front of the great monarch of the world!

That is the second feature of Paul's service
mentioned by the Lord—that he was to bear
the name of Christ before kings. Mark, it is
"the name", but what a Name! It is the
Nazarene, involving reproach, but also of Jesus
Christ, the name in which salvation is (Acts
iv. 10–12). I do not know how many kings the

apostle Paul preached to, but I do know he preached to one, and I do know too what he said to him, and I know also the spirit in which he said it, and I think it was magnificent! The spirit and substance of his address before Agrippa forms one of the finest incidents of Paul's service. He was in conscious dignity, not a dignity that he acquired at the feet of Gamaliel, or as a Pharisee of the Pharisees, but a dignity that flowed from the consciousness of his election as a minister, and of his calling as a Christian, so that he says to Agrippa "I would to God, that not only thou, but also all that hear me this day, were both almost, and altogether such as I am, except these bonds" (Acts xxvi. 29). He was the greatest in that hall; no one could compare with him; he was truly bearing the Name before kings.

Then too, the Apostle had to bear the Lord's name before the sons of Israel. These require the greatest care in the preaching. They were full of prejudice, although referred to by their Messiah in this respectful way. It is not "the Jews" here, but the "sons of Israel". How would he approach them? He would approach them, as we know he did at Antioch of Pisidia, as "Israelites", a term involving dignity, and in keeping with the Lord's reference; he was one of them and he could speak to them. But, as entering the synagogue, before addressing them, he sat down; I wish to note this because it is very practical. In the fulness of his apostolic mission he might have brushed everybody aside when he had something to say, but he sat down until he was asked to speak. It is well in service to await opportunities and not force ourselves. It is wise to wait to be asked to speak and then to address the hearers in such a manner as to inspire confidence and not provoke prejudice. Paul's manner of service at Antioch of Pisidia had good results for God.

Then the Lord also speaks of sufferings. The Lord says, "I will show to him how much he must suffer for my name". The Lord, showing him the sufferings, would not deter him from the path of devotedness.

The next feature of my subject is based on Matthew iv. 19. The Lord says, "Come after me, and I will make you fishers of men". The Lord can *make* a servant in spite of crudeness, in spite of roughness, in spite of crookedness, in spite of ignorance, in spite of prejudice— in a word, in spite of everything that attaches to an uncultured, unlettered, uninstructed, unsophisticated man—the Lord can make out of him one to whom He can give the first place in His service. Now that is Peter! I connect it with Peter because the Spirit gives us his full picture in this respect. It applies to Andrew, it applies to Paul and to every true servant, it is a second feature. It is therefore a question now of whether I am "*makeable*," for the Lord can do nothing with us whilst will is active, whilst personal motives are active, whilst prominence in the ministry is the motive. All these things stand in the way. We are told in Proverbs, "A master roughly worketh every one" (xxvi. 10), so that He can take one like Peter and make him something in His service. I would say that the Lord wishes to take each of us into His hands and make something out of us. "I will make you", He says, "fishers of men". So you find, one may say, a life-sized picture of Simon Peter, in Matthew. I think Matthew has in view the service for which the Lord intended him, that is, the circumcision, and Matthew gives us the man in his roughness and then the making process. The finished product is properly in the Acts. The Lord has great pleasure in a finished product, and I would especially speak to my young brethren here, to those who are in the making time. It is a time when the Lord is *making* servants. Each one of us may rightly ask, Am I in His hands?

You get here in chapter iv. the first mention of Peter by Matthew. He is Simon, but he is called Peter, that is to say, Matthew is looking backwards; it is the well-known Peter he is speaking about. The well-known Peter as seen in the Acts is the finished product. He is finished as a minister. The next prominent thing you get in Matthew about Peter is that he is *first*; "first . . . Peter" (chap. x. 2). He is the only one who is called first in the ministry; and if he gets that place in the Lord's mind, the making has this in view. The Lord is going to produce a minister who will occupy *that* position to His glory. "First . . . Peter", it says, and so you find in the Acts, that he is in every way first. There is nothing forced about it. If you saw Peter in his service you would discern that he had the lead among the apostles. Who made him first? The Lord. He intended him to be the leading man amongst the disciples. So you find that in the first position mentioned in the Acts, the upper room, Peter is first; and then in ministry to the brethren, Peter is first; also in preaching the gospel, Peter is first. Look at him standing up there in Jerusalem! God gave him not only the gift, but also the audience. We find there were dwelling in Jerusalem, people from almost every nation; and they are all marvelling at the effect of the Spirit's presence. There are some mocking, and Peter begins with them. Standing up with the eleven he so speaks that 3,000 were converted. Comparing the great minister seen here with the rough fisherman of Matthew iv. we may well exclaim, What hath God wrought!

So Acts shows that Peter was first, and he is so perfectly made of the Lord, that he can be in unjealous obscurity when others, like Stephen and Philip, come forward. But he is there to be called upon, which is a fine feature; hence in Acts viii. he is actually *sent* by the apostles with John. Peter and John were sent down to Samaria by the apostles that were at Jerusalem. I mention that, because it shows that whilst he was first, he was ready to be merged among his brethren, his fellow apostles, and to be subservient to them to do their bidding. That is the workmanship of Christ. How elastic, so to speak, it is in the subject of it. The body of spiritual wealth and experience seen in Peter in the later chapters of Acts is a further but most important feature of the making power of Christ in His servants.

The next thing is the lovability of the servant, and that is John. And what I would mention first about John is that he can take a *second* place. Now it is a hard thing with

some of us to do this, bu
invariably seen in that positic
beautifully—"Peter and John'
fine quality in service, to be a
second place, or, if necessary, a
Of course, in a sense, you do not w
at all, but I am speaking of the Lord's ....ring.
If Peter is first, then somebody must be second;
there are not two firsts. That is a test. So it
is "Peter and John", and I think the Lord
greatly honoured John because of this quality.
I look at him in that well-known chapter in
Acts iii., how he went up with Peter to the
temple at the hour of prayer. I suppose since
the walk of Jesus on earth, heaven never saw
anything so beautiful as that, the one that was
set "first" as the workmanship of Christ in
the service, and then the one that was second.
There they are; what a pair for heaven's eye!
It was the hour of prayer; it was the ninth
hour. Need I comment on the sentiments that
governed those two hearts as they moved up
that day to the temple at *that* hour? It was
the hour in which our Lord Jesus Christ died.
Peter says to the man, "Look on us". It was
Peter that spoke; John does not say anything.

I think John would bring forward persons
who *can be* silent in the service. It seems to me
he has in mind something of that kind in the

he mentions Lazarus. Lazarus never says anything, as far as scripture records, but in spite of this people *are believing on Jesus because of him* (John xii. 11). Now, that is a very fine thing. What kind of man must he be—he is not saying anything, and yet people are believing on Jesus because of him! Others sought to kill him because of this. The next thing you get after that is that the Lord found a colt and sat on him; the *Lord* found him. Can we not say in fairness that the Lord had Lazarus in mind when he got the colt? It was His own finding. Lazarus was the Lord's immediate product. He raised him. He was the Lord's friend. Is it not lovely to be the Lord's friend? "Our friend Lazarus", He says. Moses called his firstborn, Gershom—"I was a stranger in a strange land". That is what the world was to Jesus. He made it: "The world was made by him, and the world knew him not" (John i. 10). How strange it must have been that there was no response—but now He had a friend in it. Lazarus is a friend of Jesus in this strange place that He had to do with. I believe the conditions He found in the world caused the Lord constant sorrow; the whole scene was blighted and opposed. Every step He took aroused strange opposition. It was most unfair and uncalled for, as He says:

"They hated me without a cause" (John xv. 25). How valuable was a friend in it! That is what Lazarus was, and what the disciples were according to John: "I call you not servants . . . but I have called you friends" (John xv. 15). Wonderful, indeed, to be a friend to Jesus in a strange place like this! I wonder if all our dear young brothers and sisters look upon the world as strange, or is it just what you like and where you aspire to be? When Jesus came into it, it was a strange place to Him. Ah! it was very strange, but He found a friend and He *finds* friends. The colt He found and on which He rode into Jerusalem is in keeping with this.

Well, I am speaking of taking a second place and how one shines in it although another may be speaking. It really works out in the assembly when the brothers speak and the sisters are silent. The sisters cannot say anything, but Lazarus did not, and yet people believed on Jesus because of him. The point is not speaking; it is a question of what the person is. Sometimes in the wilderness the church is not at all lovely typically. Moses married an Ethiopian woman, and she would not be lovely. I think she is a type of some of our meetings, which are not always very lovely. Miriam and Aaron persecuted Moses because he had married the Ethiopian woman, but the Lord rebuked them and Miriam became a leper. It is a solemn thing to turn away from the brethren because they do not seem lovely to you. The Lord bears with them in their unloveliness, and you may find perhaps that your judgment is not quite right, that what you consider is unlovely is lovely in the eyes of the Lord. At any rate, if He is pleased to go on with His people I must go on with them. All this shows the importance of being lovable. In John's gospel Jesus is seen as lovable from the outset, and so Lazarus is testimony without speaking or without preaching, and that testimony is effective. It is a very important and searching word for persons who cannot speak in the assembly, and the women are enjoined not to speak there, but they are to be in such an attitude and manner and spirit that they are a testimony, and others believe on Jesus because of them.

Lovableness is the feature stressed by John in his gospel He is mentioned by name, of course, elsewhere, but he is presented in his own gospel, in this way, and that he had access to the bosom of Jesus. That is the thing; I am not preaching, I am not teaching, I am not speaking,—I am in a second position, but I have access to the bosom of Jesus, and there

I am loved by Jesus, and that is worth all the dignity, and more than all the dignity of what might accrue to us from speaking and preaching and teaching. I do not say John did not speak and preach and teach. Every one of the apostles had a gift, and every one of them used it too. You may be sure of that. In fact scripture speaks of it, that with great power "the apostles witnessed"—every one of them. After Peter and John had fulfilled their great service in Acts iii. and iv. they returned to the place of meeting, and merged among the other apostles. But John represents, as I say, the feature of lovableness and the ability to take a second place, and in that place to bear testimony, for he was, in that way, essential to Peter's service at the temple gate: "Look on *us*". The lame man would not have seen the same in Peter alone, as he saw in the two, and he discerned this, for he "held" them *both*. He held Peter and John, and on account of his presence the opposers could not say anything. He was a testimony, an evidence of the result of their testimony.

Well, that is what I had to present to you, and I commend this three-fold feature of service as converging necessarily in every servant, so that our testimony should be effective. We were seeing here this afternoon, that the mighty men of David in 1 Chronicles are mentioned immediately he is anointed king over all Israel, and they helped to establish him in the kingdom; but in 2 Samuel they come in at the end of his reign, meaning evidently in a typical way, that every mighty man from Pentecost to the coming of the Lord is included in the list. If there are to be such to-day what I have been calling attention to must have a great place with us. The Lord has gone up on high, and having led captivity captive He has given gifts to men; but there must be the qualification of the vessels. Gifts will continue to the end, and every mighty man will appear in the list. He has had something distinctive to do; every mighty man did something distinctive, and so comes into recognition as God writes up His people.

May God bless this word to us, and all that we have had before us in these meetings, for His name's sake!

SPIRITUAL MANIFESTATIONS

ADDRESS BY C. C. E.

Gen. xvii. 1, 8; xviii. 1, 6–8; Exod. xxxiv. 5–7; 1 Kings iii. 5, 9; Isa. vi. 1–3; Acts xxvi. 14–18; John xiv. 21.

I desire to speak of the reality and necessity of real spiritual experiences. It is well that we should have knowledge; it is well, too, that we should have spiritual intelligence; but what I would like to put before you is the reality of what I should name real spiritual experiences in our souls.

In all the passages I have read we find examples of this, and I refer to them in order to bring out what is latent in them. First of all, if you take Abraham, he was marked by faith, that was one of his great characteristics; but he was also marked by the number of the appearings of the Lord to him. Now, I take it none of us here is without faith. We go on in faith, if I may use the expression, with a steady tread. Day in and day out, from week to week, month to month and year to year we tread our path, I trust, in faith. To walk by faith and not by sight, is normal, surely, to all believers; and that goes on, just in a steady way daily. But what I am speaking about is something more special. I need not emphasize how important it is that we should go on day by day in this steady tread of faith, but God gives us other things; He gives us what I may speak of as appearings or manifestations, not only to confirm our faith, which is true, but to enlarge our spiritual experience. He gives us not only communications, but manifestations of Himself, and that is what we find referred to in all the passages I have read.

Abraham was a very remarkable figure in the history of God's saints, and it is said in (Gen. xii. 7) that the Lord appeared to him and said that He would give him the land. That was a remarkable appearing; the Lord confirmed Abram in leaving his country, and opened out to him His promises and, though Abram had opportunity, he never returned to the land which he had left. He accepted the result of the communication that God made to him as final, and though he may have failed at various points, yet, as the epistle to the Hebrews tells us, though he might have had opportunity to return, he did not. Abram, therefore, was confirmed in his path by this first appearing.

I read of two further appearings, one in which the name of God is declared to him: "I am the Almighty God" (Gen. xvii. 1–8). In that appearing he received great accession in regard of the name and character of God, and it was a real spiritual experience. And if he got an accession to his spiritual capital by this declaration of the name of God, his name also was changed; for that, I take it, would be a principle, that where there is a fuller revelation of the name of God, the name of the recipient of that revelation would also have a corresponding change. Thus he is now called Abraham, a change of name, corresponding to the name of God who was thus revealed to him, and vaster prospects were opened to him; he would not only have the land, but far greater blessing would accrue. What a moment for his soul to receive a revelation of that kind! God was revealed in this wonderful way, and Abram accepted it.

Then again in the other appearing of which I read (Gen. xviii.) there was even a higher privilege conferred upon Abraham, for he was placed in the position of ministering to the Holy One, of ministering refreshment to God. That is a most wonderful state of things, that Abraham should be so privileged that he should prepare a meal and minister to this blessed Visitor! Thus, in his case, there is a progression in the character, nature and extent of the intimacy of the appearings, and so it is with us. I believe that in these divine manifestations which are made to our hearts, there is a progression and increase in the character of the manifestations enjoyed. How wonderful to think that we, too, can have such manifestations of God and of the Lord Jesus to our hearts, so that we can minister to Them. How this bows our spirits in adoration and reverence before the One who so reveals Himself!

Now I come to Moses in Exodus xxxiv. Moses, who was often in touch with the Lord, here desires to see His glory, and the Lord graciously responded, and declared His name before him, and in the light of that appearing, Moses can go through the wilderness in the knowledge of God's wonderful character: "Merciful and gracious, slow to anger, and abundant in goodness and truth". God was declared in such a light as to enable Moses to carry out his heavy responsibilities, and to conduct the people of God through the wilderness under the impulse of that manifestation. I believe that every servant, in order to do any work which is entrusted to him, has to have a manifestation of the character of God or of the Lord, which will fit him for the conduct of that spiritual enterprise, however small or however great the service. If he is to serve the saints rightly, the servant must have an apprehension of the character of God which will fit him for the carrying out of what is laid upon him; and that held good with Moses. The manifestation of God in this manner just suited the character of the moment and exactly brought out what Moses required to know of God, and of the character in which he should represent God to the people. With this manifestation of God to Moses he gets also a great sense of his own insignificance, so that he could say, "Alas, this people has sinned a great sin. . . . And now, if thou wilt forgive their sin . . . but if not, blot me, I pray thee, out of thy book"; as much as to say, I do not mind about myself, let the people of God be blessed, and if my extinction will help their blessing, let my extinction take place. That would be quite in keeping with the manifestation of God, and would be the right spirit surely of a servant. So God confirms His servant in his service; He recognizes him, and Moses goes forth to that arduous service in the light of that particular manifestation of God to his soul.

Now, in regard of the next incident that I read (1 Kings iii.) that of Solomon, and the Lord appearing to him in a dream, I would point out that it was a very great thing for Solomon to recognize that the source of wisdom was in God, and that God was prepared to give it to him. I think that has a very practical bearing upon our souls; for there are occasions in which the greatest spiritual wisdom is needed. There are constantly arising difficulties amongst and regarding the Lord's people, and where are we to go? whom are we to address for the solution of those difficulties? Solomon at the outset of his career addressed the right Person and found the right source; he found in a manifest way that the wisdom he needed for ruling so great and numerous a people, was to be found in God alone, and so must we. We may take all sorts of measures and investigate all avenues, so to speak, in order to find the wisdom to meet a certain difficulty, but we are brought to the fact that wisdom comes only from God. In regard of the church it comes from her exalted Head, and all of us should have the strong impression from the Lord Himself, and from God Himself, that that is where the source of wisdom lies. So we do not act restlessly, wandering about, so to say, for guidance, much as we value the advice of our brethren through whom wisdom is often ministered to our souls; for, through whomsoever the wisdom comes, the source of it is the church's Head! What rest it gives to the spirit to know that there is no difficulty the solution of which does not lie in the mind of God, and that it is possible for us to get it!

It was surely the humble spirit in Solomon that got that answer; it was the lowly spirit that did not seek his own greatness. If there is any spirit of desiring to be great the Lord will not give us wisdom; but in the absence of that and having a pure desire to serve the Lord's people, God will give the answer.

Now there is another great effect of the manifestation of the Lord, and that would very rightly be found in a prophetic book. Isaiah said, "I saw the Lord . . . high and lifted up" (chap. vi.). What he discovered there was the holiness of God. The impression of that appearing was the extreme holiness of God; and I do verily believe that is what every one of us has to learn in a deeper way, the holiness of God and His presence which, while it attracts us, is profoundly real in its searching character. The invariable effect of the presence of God on us, is to induce an acknowledgment of the holiness that is His, and thus it banishes from us all that lightness that naturally characterises us. Lightness and the want of depth in us are banished in such measure as we are in the presence of God and have the sense of His holiness. That holiness came out in the cross is obvious; that it came out in all its deep and wonderful character there is surely known to all of us; but its realisation is one of the great points in our spiritual history, and one which has not only to be attained, but maintained.

I pass on now to the instances in the New Testament. I shall first say a word about the first great appearing of the Lord to the apostle Paul. It is one of many appearings, as the Lord said, "For this purpose have I appeared to thee to appoint thee . . . a witness both of what thou hast seen, and of what I shall appear to thee in" (Acts xxvi. 16). So there were many appearings to the apostle during his life, but this was the first, the great initial appearing. I suppose it was the greatest and it had a profound effect upon him. I have no doubt that with any servant of the Lord who seeks to serve Him, an analogous experience takes place. That is, there is a real spiritual appearing of the Lord —(not in vision like this, of course) which marks the character of the ministry. I think there is that with each of us who are servants of the Lord, and surely we all here are servants of the Lord, bondmen of Jesus Christ, and whether the work is small or great, the Lord will give us, as He gave Paul, a distinct impression of His commission. You cannot run without a commission; you cannot engage in service without a distinct impression of the Lord. It may be feeble—I do not think it was feeble with Paul—but it must be there, and that appearing will characterize the whole of the ministry of the servant.

It is very important to notice that the germ of the whole of the double ministry of Paul, is contained in what the Lord said to him here. I refer to the ministry of the church, and the ministry of the gospel. The ministry of the church is obviously contained in germ in the wonderful and beautiful expression, "Saul, Saul, why persecutest thou me? . . . I am Jesus whom thou persecutest:" We know it well. It contains the germ of the whole ministry of the church which was developed in fuller measure in Paul as he went on his course, and was the secret of all his devoted labour. If he knew and acknowledged that the church which he had persecuted was really Christ, he was prepared to prove Christ's love to the church in himself

to the utmost, whether he were loved or not:
"Though the more abundantly I love you,
the less I be loved" (2 Cor. xii. 15). He loved
and served the church which Christ loved.
That is the real motive of service to the
church; we are so impressed with Christ's
love to the church, and what the church is
to the heart of Christ, that we love to serve
it. It will prepare us for acting in the
meanest capacity, and though we may know
but little about it, it will bring suffering to us.

Now there is another feature in this appearing which I would point out, that is, the
close connection and intertwining of the two
ministries. The Lord immediately goes on to
give Paul his evangelical ministry, how he
should go to the nations to open their eyes,
"that they may turn from darkness to light,
and from the power of Satan to God". That
is the evangelical side, though without the
slightest doubt it was in view of the church,
so that those of the nations thus reached
should become part of that wonderful church
of which I have spoken. You see how the
two ministries are intertwined there; they are
not divorced; "What therefore God hath
joined together, let not man put asunder"
(Matt. xix. 6). That is, there is to be no
divorce between the ministry of the gospel

and the ministry of the church; they would
be mutually conducive to each other's pro-
gress, and they are both impressed upon the
apostle at this wonderful appearing.

I have already referred to the many appearings that were made to Paul, and of some we
have a record. For instance, when he came
to Jerusalem and wanted to stay there and
preach, the Lord appeared to him in a trance
and said, "Get thee quickly out of Jerusalem"
(Acts xxii. 18). He pleaded with the Lord,
and said he would like to stay: "Lord, they
know that I imprisoned and beat in every
synagogue them that believed on thee: And
when the blood of thy martyr Stephen was
shed, I also was standing by, and consenting
unto his death, and kept the raiment of them
that slew him". But the Lord became insistent
and said, You are to go. The Lord is able to
appear to His servants to give them directions
for service, and while we may have to gather
much as to His will, there is such a thing
as the Lord giving peremptory instructions,
and I suppose every servant knows what that
is; you cannot argue; you *must* do it.

That was the result of one appearing of
the Lord to Paul; and, again, when the apostle
was in some distress because he had made an
error before the council, that very night the

gracious Lord stood by him and said, "Be of good cheer, Paul: for as thou hast testified of me in Jerusalem, so must thou bear witness also at Rome" (Acts xxiii. 11). He would fulfil his service, and he would go to Rome and testify for the Lord there. The Lord is so gracious; He knew that the heart and the motive were right, and He would comfort His servant.

Then again, we read that after he had been caught up to the third heaven, which was indeed more than an appearing, when he came down he was given the thorn in the flesh, and found it very trying for himself, a man of so impetuous and active a character. He besought the Lord thrice to take it from him, but the Lord said, "My grace is sufficient for thee: for my strength is made perfect in weakness" (2 Cor. xii. 9). So he was called to suffer this, that he might find the power of Christ resting upon him. That was a gracious, comforting word of the Lord to him, and showed what a deep interest the Lord took in His servant, and how His grace was sufficient for this and every thing of that kind.

When again at the end of his arduous life of service he stands before that inhuman monster whom he calls "the lion", and all the saints at Rome, who seem to have been very timid, deserted him, and no man stood by him, the Lord again manifested Himself to him, as he says, "The Lord stood by me" (2 Tim. iv. 17). Do you think the Lord would desert His servant though all deserted him? Never; He made Himself known in full support to His servant. Oh! do we not feel it, that it is only as He supports us that we have courage? It is only as He supports us that service is at all effectual, so that, as he says, "by me the preaching might be fully known". But He does support us, as He supported His aged servant at that moment. We see thus how Paul was well acquainted with these wonderful manifestations and communications from the Lord.

Now in the last passage I read (John xiv.) we have a different note. We should expect the apostle John to present things to us in a character corresponding to his ministry, and thus we find here the character of the manifestations of the Lord from John's aspect. "He that hath my commandments, and keepeth them, he it is that loveth me: and he that loveth me shall be loved of my Father, and I will love him, and will manifest myself to him". This then is a manifestation of affection. I do not mean that the others were not given in affection, but the stress here is laid upon affection, so that the manifestation is really one of pure affection. It is not a manifestation here for service, but a manifestation for affection: "He that loveth me shall be loved of my Father, and I will love him, and will manifest myself to him".

Now, that is a real spiritual experience. Would to God we knew more about it! And I may say that it is not a bit of use reading this beautiful passage of scripture and never experiencing the truth of it. I believe there are many believers who constantly admire and find comfort in this chapter, but who have not really experienced what this verse speaks about. But it is open to us. You say, How is it open to us? Love obeys, and that is how it is opened to us: "He that hath my commandments, and keepeth them". So it is by the simple way of obedience. I do not know what you find, but I find in myself there is a great danger of not being simply obedient to the Lord. We may not be distinctly, directly and completely obedient to what the Lord tells us, and that is why we do not get these manifestations, for do you mean to tell me for one moment that love does not desire to bestow this favour? Of course it does. Do you mean to say that the Lord does not wish to manifest Himself to each of us? Of course He does, and the only thing that prevents Him, I believe, is our lack of obedience; but if obedience is there, and we love Him, He will certainly manifest Himself to us.

Now we may know a little about it or may know a great deal about it, but one feels we should all be exercised as to our experience of these things. Opposers say there is nothing in it but mere imagination; but manifestations of the Lord are real; and what is the effect in the soul? It is that the love of Christ is very near to us, very warm in our hearts, and we greatly appreciate it and enjoy it. I cannot explain its effects better than that. There is a realization of His love in a deeper sense than ever. And if I may refer to the collective thought, I believe the same holds good. We should never be content with a mere description of things, but we should realize when He comes to us. Not that we can claim it in a public way, but nevertheless the reality remains, and it should be our happy privilege, not only that we should read about it, but that we should experience it.

I do believe it is of the utmost importance that such spiritual experiences as I have referred to, should be known by every one of us, and, if what I have said tends to send us to the Lord in prayer to see what it is that prevents them being ours, I shall be glad indeed. As this chapter (John xiv.) shows us, faith, however great, is not enough. It says, "Ye believe on God, believe also on me", and that, I understand, we all do. We all do believe on Him, there is faith, and that gets us over our difficulties and makes us go on so that we do not lose heart. As I said before, it keeps us going on steadily; but the Lord would have us enjoy more than that, namely the manifestations of Himself to our hearts, whether in love, or in any other of the aspects presented in these scriptures, for I have touched but the fringe of the subject. Let us then earnestly seek them in the power of the Spirit given to us, with the knowledge that all these experiences are possible for us, if we are exercised. May they become the real experience of our souls for His name's sake.

SUBJECTION

ADDRESS BY W. J. H.

2 Thess. ii. 7, 8; Luke i. 38; ii. 1–7; 1 Cor. xv. 24–28.

WHAT I want to suggest, beloved brethren, is the importance of subjection; and, with the Lord's help, I would desire to indicate that, if we are to be in accord with the mind of God in any relationship or position in which God has set us, or if we are to be prepared for that eternity that lies ahead into which we are about to enter, subjection is imperative as a state that is wrought in our souls; not simply that as to certain actions, we obey, but that the spring of those actions, is a state of subjection that exists in our souls. One feels the importance of it more because of the intensely solemn moment in which our lot is cast in this world. Without doubt we are rapidly drawing near to the moment that I read of in the epistle to the Thessalonians, when one will be revealed whom the Spirit of God calls by name—"*the* lawless one", or, as our ordinary version gives it, "that Wicked". There is about to appear the great leader,

whose characteristic feature and name is lawlessness, and the darkening influences that will
reach a climax with his presence on earth,
are already here. The smoke of the pit out
of which he comes—for it says that he ascends
out of the bottomless pit—is already filling the
earth, darkening every right influence that has
hitherto governed the minds of men, affecting
every relationship where subjection is proper.

In the wisdom of God, from our very birth,
we are brought into a position in which subjection is the first feature. As children, the
mind of God for children is subjection. The
influence of the lawless one is being felt intensely in that relationship. Those of us who
have children feel intensely the darkening
there. Then, if I refer just for a moment to
women, the mind of God for the woman is
subjection to the man; but the influence of
the lawless one from the pit, is breaking that
down. Again, as to the wife, her place according to the mind of God, is subjection to her
own husband, that too, is being destroyed.
The principle of subjection to the higher
powers, is the mind of God in respect of government; it is being undermined everywhere. The
principle of subjection of the servant to his
master, is being abandoned everywhere. I
need not say that that which professes to be

the church, is manifestly abandoning that subjection. The awful influences of lawlessness are darkening this scene, and God, I am sure, would save us from it, by conveying to our hearts the blessedness of subjection, not that we accept it as inevitable, but that we accept it as *loving* it.

Hence I would desire to speak of Christ,— the blessed One in whom every thought of God for men, finds perfect expression. As the Lord said, "Take my yoke upon you, and learn from me". Whatever we may consider, everything is expressed perfectly, and can only be learnt perfectly from Christ. Thus I desire, with the Lord's help, to seek to present subjection, as it is seen in its blessed perfection in Christ, so that, as seeing it in Him, we may learn to love it, and thus get the gain that it brings.

I know that certain features of subjection were expressed here, in measure, before He came; but one loves to think that everything that has been right and of God was but the backward glow of the rising sun. As the sun comes up and we get the present shining of it, there still remain the beams of light that go backward, and every feature that was of God, from Abel onward, was really the beaming of that blessed light, that *great light* that the Lord speaks of: "The people sitting in darkness has seen a great light" (Matt. iv. 16). The beams of that light went backward, so that everything that was of God from Abel forward, was a ray of that light. The apostle Peter speaks of it, "The Spirit of Christ which was in them" (1 Peter. i. 11), not that we imply it was there, or read it into it, but it *was* there; the Spirit of Christ was there "in them". So, if Abel was marked by subjection, which lies behind the Lord calling him "righteous Abel", it was that which he derived from Christ; and if Abraham was subject to the divine command "Get thee out of thy country, and from thy kindred, and from thy father's house", he went out as subject. To Moses God said, "my servant Moses"; and of David He said, "I have found David my servant"; these were men who were subject to God as having the Spirit of Christ. But I wanted just to indicate as the Lord may give grace, some sense of the perfection of subjection as seen in Christ Himself.

So, if we come to the outset of His entrance into time, it is as One who was "from eternity", of whom the Spirit of God speaks as "being in the form of God". What infinite greatness! Subjection does not apply to the form of God, I need not say; it is for God to command.

Innumerable hosts of angels are before Him, as it says, "hearkening unto the voice of his word" (Psa. ciii. 20), bending their ears, awaiting the divine command. Of Gabriel it says, "I am Gabriel, that stand in the presence of God", but the form of God has never been seen, and never will be seen, by a creature: "Dwelling in unapproachable light; whom no man has seen, nor is able to see; to whom be honour and eternal might. Amen." (1 Tim. vi. 16.) But the One who was in the form of God, took a servant's form. Our hearts cannot take that in. "Subsisting in the form of God", it says He took—it was a deliberate, definite act—"a bondman's form". He *took* a condition in which subjection could be perfectly expressed. The setting of the passage in Philippians is primarily, that the mind was there to do it, before the act was consummated. The apostle says, "Let this mind be in you which was also in Christ Jesus". It was firstly, an act of mind, to take a servant's form, to come into a condition where subjection could be expressed, to accept the absolute will of God,—for that is the idea of a bondman. A bondman is not at liberty to act for himself; a bondman is bound by the will of his master. The word "master" in some places, means despot; it means one who will not brook, who will not tolerate another will. The Lord Jesus took a bondman's form and was found in fashion as a Man.

Who is there that is suited for the coming in of Christ? What vessel is there that God will use as prepared under His own mighty hand of power, for the entrance of such a One into the world? One indeed, of whom it is said "Lo, *I come* . . . to do thy will, O God". The Spirit of God selects a certain vessel for this supremely great act, when He should take a "bondman's form" and be "found in figure as a man". (Phil. ii. 7, 8.) Who is it? The verse I read indicates the suitability of Mary to be such a vessel. She says, "Behold the bondmaid of the Lord". She corresponded subjectively, with the mind that had decided to take a bondman's form, the bondmaid corresponding with the Bond-man. "Behold the bondmaid of the Lord; be it to me according to thy word". There was in that beloved woman's soul, wrought in it subjectively, subjection to the will of God.

Then the Lord Jesus Himself is born as Joseph and Mary are in the very act of expressing subjection, according to the mind of God. The decree as to the census had gone forth from Cæsar Augustus, the alien power that then was, a decree naturally irritant to the heart of any Jew, but recognising the power God had ordained, Joseph and Mary, at cost to themselves that we cannot fully understand, carried out in subjection God's mind in relation to the higher powers; and at that very moment the Lord Jesus is found here in this scene, in the very atmosphere and conditions of subjection.

He moves from that point, and we next see Him at twelve years of age, a solemn age,—an age that is testing perhaps more than most. The Lord says to Mary consequent upon those twelve years in secret, "Did ye not know that I ought to be occupied in my Father's business?" He assumes that she would have understood in those twelve years, how imperative it was for Him to be subject to the will of God, that His Father's business should control and govern Him. Nevertheless, at that very moment it says that He went down to Nazareth and was "subject unto them",—expressing perfectly from twelve years and onward, the mind of God during that period. It says, He "was subject unto them". What days they were,—the eye and heart of God alone can put an estimate upon them! Then He "began to be about thirty years of age", indicating what those days of subjection were to God, for He says, at the close of them, "Thou art my beloved Son, in thee I have found my delight"; not "I do find" though that would be true, but "I have". God had looked upon every one of those days, and the divine estimate is expressed of what that subjection in secret and obscurity was to Him: "in thee, I have found my delight".

But then we follow Him during those three and a half years, and it is indicated that they are taken account of in days. The Spirit of God suggests in the book of Daniel, a period like them, in which every one of them is remembered: "Blessed is he that waiteth, and cometh to the thousand three hundred and thirty-five days" (xii. 12). The days are taken account of, every one of them, and all were days of subjection. They were begun in a way that makes one feel intensely humbled when we compare our days with His. How many of us must feel like Jacob, "few and evil have been the days of the years of my pilgrimage", but that does not in any wise represent those blessed days of His! They may have been few, as men count days—but they were infinitely blessed! They were begun each morning in subjection, as it says, "He wakeneth morning by morning, he wakeneth mine ear to hear as the instructed" (Isa. l. 4). Think of that, beloved brethren; every single day, morning by morning, His ear was opened for instruction. It is the Bondman waiting upon His Master whom He loved for instructions for the day. Every single day was like that! No wonder the memorial of them is laid up before God; no wonder that the Lord said that the time would come when men would look to see *one* of those days—just one! If it be that the instruction for one day was that "He must needs go through Samaria"—albeit that the journey brings weariness to Him,—there is no question of *His* subjection,—so that at that very moment He says, "My meat is to do the will of him that sent me".

What shall we say of the closing day of those days? One can only remind you of what has been said:

"O day of mightiest sorrow,
    Day of unfathomed grief;
When Thou shouldst taste the horror
    Of wrath, without relief:"—

that was the last day of the sojourn of Christ here. See Him at the commencement of it, in prayer for instruction, knowing perfectly what that day contained in His own spirit,— shrinking from it in a holiness that we adore, yet nevertheless asking for instructions: "O

my Father, if it be possible, let this cup pass
from me: nevertheless not as *I* will, but as
thou wilt". What subjection! We cannot view
it save "a stone's throw" away; not even
Peter or James or John could go all the way
to contemplate it. He went a stone's throw
beyond any point that they could go. But we
see subjection in perfection there, as always.
And so He dies: He lays down His life in
subjection. One point of view of the death
of Christ beyond and outside of the instruments that caused it, is, that He laid down
His life in subjection: "I have received this
commandment of my Father." His death was
the supreme act of subjection.

One used to think that that act was the end
of subjection in Christ, and that ever after it
would be rule, it would be command. But,
dear brethren, that is not so. Having entered
into manhood, He *retains* manhood in subjection. One view of the resurrection, of His
taking His life again in manhood, is, that it
is done in subjection: "I have authority to lay
it down and I have authority to take it again.
I have received this commandment of my
Father" (John x. 18). The commandment
covers both the laying it down and the taking
it again. Commanded to take it again in
resurrection, obedience to that command is

expressed in His resurrection. I do not of
course refer to that point we love to take
account of, that it was the surpassing greatness of the power of *God* that wrought in
Christ in raising Him from the dead, but
there is also this view in John x. 18, that
He took it again in subjection to a divine
command.

Our thoughts and our hearts would go to
the passage we read in 1 Corinthians xv. His
present position is "Sit thou at my right hand,
until I make thine enemies thy footstool"; sit
there till every single thing is subject to Christ.
That is the mind of God for Christ at the
present moment. As Pharaoh said to Joseph;
"I am Pharaoh", "only in the throne, will
I be greater than thou", but otherwise no one
was to lift their hand or foot without Joseph.
That is the position of Christ, and it will continue until everything is subject to Him. God
is going to put *everything* in subjection to Christ,
and when everything is subdued, when there
is nothing unsubdued in the universe of God,—
what then? It is beyond *us* to express,—but
the Spirit of God says when everything shall
have been brought into subjection to Him,
then "the Son also himself shall be placed
in subjection" (verse 28). We are now in our
thoughts touching a little on what we have

had before us—"to eternity"; "from eternity, to eternity". That passage in 1 Corinthians xv. brings us, as it were, to the door of eternity. What place will the Son have in eternity? One would not dare to say it, if the Spirit of God in the Scripture did not say it, but the Son will be placed, not exactly He will *become* subject, as by His own act, though that would be true,—but He is *placed by God* in subjection. The Son, the One whom the Father loves, for "the Father loves the Son"—that One who has made God known to our hearts, is placed in subjection by God. The One whom we all love to kiss even to-day, for it says, "Kiss the Son": the One towards whom the holy affections of the liberated universe will yet express themselves,—of Him it says, "the Son also himself shall be placed in subjection". The underlying condition of all eternity is subjection to God: "from eternity to eternity, thou art God". Subjection will be the basic condition of the universe eternally. There is an aspect of God's kingdom that is eternal, as the apostle says, "Now unto the King eternal, immortal, invisible, the only wise God, be honour and glory for ever and ever. Amen". (1 Tim. i. 17.) That will be secured to God for ever, as the Son remains for ever in manhood, in subjection to God.

Now, if we are to get the gain of what is in the mind of God for us, there must be subjection. You can see that in the gospel of John, where the Lord comes into the time condition and scene out of eternity. "In the beginning was the Word, and the Word was with God, and the Word was God". Then further, "the Word became flesh, and dwelt among us". What will He not bring in? What will not such a One bring in as available to men? Who could measure it? No one. The apostle says, "for of his fulness we all have received, and grace upon grace" because of *Who* had come in. But who got the gain of what He brought in? Those who were subject. Take the good wine,—the joy that is never deficient, joy that will continue for ever,—who got it? Those who were subject. Mary for the moment, beloved woman whom all generations call blessed, stepped out of the place of subjection, and said to Him, "They have no wine". She undertook to direct *Him*, but the Lord will not allow that, and she accepts the adjustment. She is a woman who can be adjusted, and she says, "Whatever he may say to you, do". That is subjection. The Lord says, "Fill the waterpots with water", and they filled them. "Draw out now", and they drew out. The lawless mind would have said, Why fill them with water? and, What is the use of drawing them out? But there was subjection, and the good wine was there. Beloved brethren, we only know what the good wine is, as we are subject. And so in chapter iv., the nobleman's son is ill and about to die, and he comes to the Lord knowing by faith that because of who He was, He could bring in what was needed, and the Lord says, "Go thy way, thy son liveth"; and we read that he went his way. There was subjection, and healing flows from subjection. If there are conditions that require healing, and there are such everywhere,—healing comes in where there is subjection. In chapter vi., where it is a question of food, you have the same principle coming to light. Five thousand men are there, and what does the Lord say? "Make the men sit down". There is acceptance in subjection of what the Lord says, and the food comes; it comes where there is subjection. In chapter ix. you have the same principle. There is a man born blind and in darkness, but the Lord makes clay and puts it on his eyes, and says to him, "Go, wash in the pool of Siloam" which is, "Sent", and the man went, and washed, and came seeing. Does not that touch the question why some of us do not see? Someone recently said, As long as I live I will

not accept that—speaking in regard to light
the Lord had given. Could he ever see?
Never; till there is subjection, but where there
is that, the light will come. It involves subjection not only to the Lord, but as Peter says,
"Likewise, ye younger, submit yourselves unto
the elder" (1 Peter v. 5). That does not
refer merely to years, but to those who have
known God longer and better than we. The
word is to submit, and light comes where
there is subjection. Peter goes on to say,
"Yea, all of you be subject one to another",
and that is a basic condition for light to come.
The Lord said, "Go," and the man says,
"I went;" the Lord said, "Wash," and he
says, "I washed and do see;" there was subjection.

Again just one more word. The Lord Jesus
appears at the grave of Lazarus. Mary and
Martha, with a right sense of what such a
One as John's gospel presents, could do, sent
for Him, but the Lord remained where He
was two days,—deliberately allowing the condition to fully manifest itself, and then He
went. He comes to the grave, and there was
a stone upon it, and the Lord says, Take away
the stone. Martha says, No, do not allow the
awful condition there to be manifest; hide it.
But the Lord says, "Take away the stone," and

it says, "They took therefore the stone away."
Where darkness and corruption have been,
life and incorruptibility are brought to light.
It is life out of death, only known where there
is subjection. We cannot have living conditions without subjection. How often we are
like Martha, we shrink from allowing the
Lord to uncover, or have uncovered, the condition which exists, and which He knows
better than we do, but if He uncovers the
conditions, it is but to manifest His power,
when there is subjection.

May the Lord help us all, not only to
accept the principle of subjection as ordained
of God for us,—but that we may *love* it, as
seeing its beauty and perfection in Christ, and
as knowing it is to continue through all eternity—the eternity that is before us. Subjection
to God will remain unbroken throughout all
eternity, but we will get the gain of what is
eternal *now*, in the measure in which we are
prepared to be subject. May the Lord thus
help us.